1. Banff Springs Hotel
2. Chateau Lake Louise
   Plain of Six Glaciers Teahouse
3. Jasper Park Lodge
4. Prince of Wales Hotel
5. Emerald Lake Lodge
6. Lake O'Hara Lodge
7. Num-Ti-Jah
8. Twin Falls Chalet
9. Abbott Pass Hut
10. Skoki Lodge
11. Mt. Assiniboine Lodge
12. Shadow Lake Lodge

Map of Great Lodges of the Canadian Rockies

To Hal,

For blazing my trail
through the Rockies,

Thanks & best wishes,

Christie Reamer

Oct. 2, 1999

# Great Lodges
## of the Canadian Rockies

By Christine Barnes

Photography by Fred Pflughoft & David Morris

W.W. WEST

*Above: In the northern reaches of the Rockies, on the shores of Lac Beauvert, stands the Jasper Park Lodge complex.*
*Title page: The main lounge of Num-Ti-Jah Lodge, Banff National Park.*

For
Basil Gardom,
in memoriam

## Acknowledgments

The author wishes to thank all of the historians, librarians, archivists, and individuals who helped uncover the past, especially: Brian Patton for his constant encouragement, assistance and good humor; Nancy Williatte-Battet; Don Bourdon, Lena Goon, E.J. Hart & the staff of The Whyte Museum of the Canadian Rockies; Jim Bowman; Joanne Cordis; The Honourable Garde B. Gardom, Q.C., Lieutenant-Governor of British Columbia; Sonya Littledeer; Jim Taylor; Sophie Tellier; Jon Whelan and W.B. "Bill" Yeo.

To those affiliated with the hotels and lodges, among them Alison Brewster and Byran Niehaus, Annette and Bud Brewster, Kerry Busby, Fran Drummond, Janet Eger, Rosemarie Enslin, Laszlo Funtek, Samantha Geer, Jean-Claude Guenat, Ken Jones, Joy Kimball, Robert LeBlond, Alison and Bruce Millar, Sue Moore, Blake O'Brian, Pat O'Connor, Lee O'Donnell, Barb and Sepp Renner, R.W. Sandford, Jimmy Simpson, Jr., Tim Whyte and Holly J. Wood.

My family and friends, most importantly, Jerry, Melissa, Sanjay, Michael, Karen, Deborah and my parents. And Don Compton for his continued support.

❖

First Printing

Copyright © 1999 Text by Christine Barnes
Copyright © 1999 Photographers Credited
Published by W.W. West, Inc. 20875 Sholes Road, Bend, Oregon 97702

Book design, railroad illustration & map: Linda McCray
Lodge illustration: Dave Ember
Copy editor: Barbara Fifer

**Publisher's Cataloging-in-Publication Data
(prepared by Quality Books, Inc.)**

Barnes, Christine, 1947-
    Great Lodges of the Canadian Rockies / by
Christine Barnes , photographs by Fred Pfugholft &
David Morris. -- 1st ed.
    p. cm.
    Includes bibliographical references and index.
    ISBN: 0-9653924-2-2      LCCN: 99-70805

    1. Architecture--Canadian Rockies (B.C. and Alta.) 2.
Architecture, Modern--20th century--Canadian Rockies (B.C.
and Alta.) 3. Historical buildings--Canadian Rockies (B.C. and
Alta.) 4. Hotels--Canadian Rockies (B.C. and Alta.) 5. Canadian
Rockies (B.C. and Alta.)--Description and travel. 1. Title.

NA7850.C3B37 1999                    728.5'0971'1
                    QB199-99

Printed in Hong Kong by C&C Offset Printing Co., LTD.

*The verandah dining room of Emerald Lake Lodge, Yoho National Park.*

# Contents

*On November 7, 1885, Donald A. Smith drove the last spike in the Canadian Pacific Railway's line across Canada.*

# ALL ABOARD! *Castles, Cabins, Parks, People & Promotion*

The Great Lodges of the Canadian Rockies forever will be linked to one of the most audacious political and engineering feats in North American history.

The Canadian Parliament had withstood the longest debate in its history—nearly ten years—when on February 1, the Canadian Railway Bill of 1881 was finalized. An ill and fatigued Prime Minister Sir John A. Macdonald would need six months of rest to regain his health from the ordeal. Other ranking politicians had been scandalized and humiliated, their reputations, health and businesses ruined.

But when all was said and done, the Canadian Pacific Railway Company was a reality, and the impact it would have on Canada would be unmatched. The bill gave the Canadian Pacific $25 million, a land grant of 25 million acres along the right-of-way (including tax exemption), a waiver of duties on importing material for construction plus a twenty-year monopoly on transportation from the Prairies into the United States. What Canada would get in return was a transcontinental rail line to be completed in ten years.

The CPR syndicate was run by a group of savvy, successful and driven men: Donald A. Smith, a native of Scotland, who had made his reputation with the Hudson's Bay Company; his cousin, George Stephen, a financier associated with the Bank of Montreal; and James Hill, a Canadian-born transportation baron who made his fortune in the United States. It was Hill who bullied strongest for the southern route of the CPR to be built through the Rocky Mountains, thus through the most spectacular mountain scenery in North America. And it was Hill who then had the job of finding a man to match the enormous task ahead of the company. He selected William Cornelius Van Horne to fulfill the Canadian Pacific Railway's deal to provide a train line that would pull together the massive hulk of Canada.

In 1882, American-born Van Horne crossed the border and pledged his allegiance to the Dominion and the CPR with as much brash vigor as, say, Donald Trump might in a modern scenario. With a background as general manager of the Chicago, Milwaukee and St. Paul Railroad, Van Horne was hardly a neophyte when it came to challenging tasks. With him as the Canadian Pacific's new vice-president and general manager, the railway laid a strap across Canada that forever changed—and united—the young nation.

Native peoples had long ago found manageable routes across the rugged and untamed Rocky Mountains. Fur traders and explorers following in their footsteps saw the mountains as obstacles, difficult and treacherous barriers obstructing their commercial quests.

By 1881, expedition and survey parties had been braving the uncharted range for decades. Survey competition was hot, heated and hostile over which

**Banff**

A **CANADIAN PACIFIC HOTEL** IN THE **CANADIAN ROCKIES**

*The CPR's beautifully illustrated brochures enticed visitors to the elegant Banff Springs Hotel and other attractions of the Canadian Rockies.*

route was best suited for the rail line. Early on, the government favored crossing the Rockies over Yellowhead Pass west of Jasper, and the CPR surveyed the area between 1872 and 1875. But James Hill declared in the spring of 1881: "Gentlemen, we will cross the prairie and go by the Bow [Kicking Horse] Pass, if we can get that way."

"Getting that way" was one of the great hurdles in railway history. Major A.B. Rogers, the notoriously cantankerous, Yale-educated railway engineer, is credited with finding the final pass across the Selkirks that would complete the line through the Rockies.

The tracks through the Selkirk and Rocky mountains were built by hundreds of men following the surveys of those whose names many peaks and passes now bear. But responsibility for completion of the line was firmly placed on the shoulders of Van Horne.

On November 7, 1885, the last spike of the railway's transcontinental line was driven near Craigellachie, British Columbia.

That line cut its way through the most stunning mountains in North America through the Bow Valley over Kicking Horse Pass and to Rogers Pass. To Van Horne, the towering crags and remarkable vistas were a business opportunity. "Since we can't export the scenery," he said, "we shall have to import the tourists." His enthusiasm for tourism was shared by the railway and the Canadian government.

By the 1880s, the upper and affluent classes of Europe and North America had been struck by wanderlust. "Grand tours" and leisurely visits to spa resorts were the rage. A hardier group of English tourists became fascinated with mountain climbing and alpine hiking. Beginning in 1863, Englishman Thomas Cook began offering package tours to the Swiss Alps. Certainly, the U.S. and Canadian Rocky Mountains were as challenging and spectacular as their Swiss counterparts. More importantly, these peaks offered virgin territory to those lusting for first ascents. Unlike in Europe, great expanses of land had to be crossed in order to wallow in the wild beauty of these mountain destinations.

Rail travel and the new comforts afforded tourists in Pullman and dining cars opened up remote regions of both the Canadian and American wilderness. Overseas clientele traveled from Europe after 1900 via the CPR's own fleet of liners and plied the Pacific on CPR ships in the 1890s. The Canadian railways also developed connections with American transcontinental lines making the Canadian mountains a natural extension for tourists attracted to the wilderness of the Western United States.

## Parks and People

The U.S. government set aside huge plots of stunning land beginning with Yellowstone National Park in 1872. While its interests were primarily in

*William Cornelius Van Horne, the CPR's first general manager, was instrumental in creating tourism in the Canadian Rockies.*

preservation and conservation, business interests were promoting the parks. The Great Northern, Union Pacific and Santa Fe railways were among those champing at the bit to deliver passengers and reap profits from U.S. national parks tourism. American railways eventually built lines to and constructed great lodges in many of the parks beginning with Old Faithful Inn (1904) in Yellowstone. But in Canada, where railway and government interests were linked at the onset, large-scale resort development flourished. That private and public partnership, sealed in Ottawa in 1881, was meant to generate revenue from the costly CPR line through the mountains.

Sir Sandford Fleming, engineer-in-chief of the CPR and an avid alpinist, proposed the idea of parks along the railway's mountain route in 1883. Van Horne was in full agreement. The Canadian government would reserve the scenic land and develop the recreational facilities, and the railway would transport tourists to the parks and provide dining and lodging. A small park reserve was established around recently discovered hot springs in the Bow Valley in November 1885, then enlarged and named Rocky Mountains Park in 1887. Prime Minister Macdonald addressing Parliament in April 1887 emphasized the monetary and scenic attributes of establishing the Park: "I do not suppose in any portion of the world there can be found a spot…which combines so many attractions and which promises in as great a degree not only large pecuniary advantage to the Dominion, but much prestige to the whole country by attracting the population, not only of this continent, but of Europe to this place."

## Let the Building Begin

The government laid out a townsite near the springs, leasing lots for homes and businesses that provided for the needs of tourists and generated funds for the federal government. As for the railway, they had already begun building the Banff Springs Hotel, a resort that would dwarf any previous mountain stations.

The first accommodations along the CPR line were constructed for practical purpose. While the spine of tracks stretched over the mountains, the steam locomotives hauling them were no match for the dining cars in tow. Dining stations were built—Mount Stephen House at Field, Glacier House near Rogers Pass and Fraser Canyon Hotel at North Bend, all in British Columbia— offering passengers a respite from the rail trip. As travelers began to leave the shelter of the train cars and enjoy short treks around dining stations, they wanted to stay longer. The dining stations, with a few rooms for staff and some guests, were soon expanded into hotels.

Montreal architect Thomas Charles Sorby submitted plans for the three dining stations in November 1885, and they were built during the following two years. Each featured a three-story core, two-story wing to one side, and one-story dining hall on the other. Their verandahs, upstairs dormers and wood trim offered a simple yet picturesque design in keeping with the mountain setting.

Glacier House was the most popular stop due to its lovely location near the Illecillewaet Glacier. In 1890-1892 an annex was built with thirty-two bedrooms and additional sitting-rooms, based on the 1889 design by Bruce Price. In 1902, a fifty-four-room wing was designed by Francis Mawson Rattenbury. Rattenbury, who was simultaneously submitting substantial revisions for CPR's Vancouver Hotel (a Sorby design), also designed two additions at Mount Stephen House. In each addition, he shifted from the original Sorby plan. Whether with Tudor wings or shingled English Arts & Crafts additions, he used turrets, observation towers, and verandahs to transform the dining stations to hotel status.

None of these survives today, but Sorby, Price and Rattenbury played significant roles in the CPR's growing hotel development in the mountains, and in Canada's cities as well.

The CPR's mountain architecture evolved, drawing from the Canadian Chateau style of its cosmopolitan hotels, and used Shingle, Tudor, mountain chalet and rustic designs. The railway constructed the Banff Springs Hotel (1888) and Lake Louise Chalet (1890), later transformed into Chateau Lake Louise. The two major hotels were in a constant state of change, in part due to devastating fires.

By 1902, the flood of hotel construction warranted additional management, and the CPR created a hotel department.

The Canadian Pacific Railway was not the only train line in Canada. In 1903, the National Transcontinental Railway Act awarded an alternative national rail route to the Grand Trunk Pacific Railway and the Canadian Northern Railway. Tracks were laid west from Edmonton to the Athabasca Valley and crossed the more northern portion of the Rockies.

Following the CPR's lead, Grand Trunk executives saw the economic potential in creating parks along the railway's scenic routes. They lobbied for a federal reserve, and in 1907, 5,000 square miles along the Athabasca River were set aside. But the Grand Trunk was mired in financial and political problems. The Grand Trunk and Canadian Northern railways merged, and the publicly-owned Canadian National Railway was born.

It wasn't until the early 1920s that the CNR, under the direction of visionary president Sir Henry Thornton, built sprawling Jasper Park Lodge and Bungalow Camp on Lac Beauvert at the site of a successful camp "Tent City."

Jasper Park Lodge did not embrace the chateau architecture favored by the CPR. Instead, the CNR used logs and stone, creating Canada's version of the lodges in America's national parks and Adirondacks camps in upstate New York. The public loved the elegant camp idea, and eventually the resort would be transformed into the largest group of recreational log buildings on the continent.

In Waterton Lakes National Park, the Great Northern Railway, founded by James Hill, built the Prince of Wales Hotel in 1927 as an extension of the American railway's Glacier National Park development in Montana. Motor coaches carried guests between Waterton and Banff.

*The elegant Banff Springs Hotel, along the railway's line and within Canada's first national park, was the first luxury hotel in the wilds of the Canadian Rockies, circa 1910.*

*The CPR promoted the Rockies as a Canadian version of the Swiss Alps and hired Swiss guides to lead climbers up the spectacular peaks.*

## Backcountry & Bungalow Camps

While Banff Springs Hotel, Chateau Lake Louise, Jasper Park Lodge and the Prince of Wales Hotel comprise the largest historic lodges in the Canadian Rockies, big does not always mean better.

The Canadian Pacific Railway never rested. The CPR built the Swiss-inspired Emerald Lake Chalet in Yoho National Park beginning in 1902-04.

Spurred by tourists' demands for accommodations in the far reaches of the Rockies, a series of tent camps was set up. Many of these evolved into log bungalow camps, beginning in a meadow near Lake O'Hara, also in Yoho. One of the world's great hiking and riding trail systems was cut into the backcountry linking these sites.

Swiss guides had been hired by the CPR to lead climbing parties from its hotels beginning in 1899 when Edward Feuz, Sr., and Christian Häsler, Sr., both of Interlaken, were stationed at Glacier House. By 1912, guides and their families settled near Golden, British Columbia in a "Swiss" village built by the CPR.

Not only were the guides instrumental in opening up the peaks to climbers, but also they were keen on having huts and shelters built for parties making ascents. The first hut for climbers was on Rogers Pass (1904); the most famous is Abbot Hut on Abbot Pass (1923).

Following World War I, motor tourists began to outnumber rail tourists in the mountain parks. Besides arriving in their own vehicles, this new tourist segment preferred less formal and more flexible accommodations than the well-heeled and more formally attired rail tourists. In order to tap this emerging market, the CPR introduced the bungalow camp. Basil Gardom, the CPR's innovative and tireless superintendent of construction and repairs for the western hotels, developed and executed the bungalow camp concept. A bungalow camp boom took place from 1919 to 1928.

Gardom, a rugged outdoorsman, emigrated to Canada from England when he was seventeen, settling in Enderby in the Okanagan Valley of British Columbia. There he cleared and drained land and built his own log cabin, an experience that would bode well for his later career. His selection of simple log cabins clustered in camps in the Canadian Rockies filled the wilderness fantasies tourists longed for, creating retreats in keeping with their settings.

Each camp featured a main lodge for cooking, dining and socializing, surrounded by individual guest cabins. CPR bungalow camps were links in a well-planned and executed Bungalow Camp Tour through the national parks. Gardom began building with Lake O'Hara Camp and Moraine Lake Camp.

New and improved roads through the parks prompted construction of Wapta Lake Camp, Castle Mountain, Vermilion River Bungalow Camp, Windermere Camp, Sinclair Hot Springs Camp and Yoho Bungalow Camp. In addition, Lake O'Hara and Emerald Lake Chalet were expanded into deluxe bungalow camps. Along with these, tea houses and rest houses added to the expanding camp network.

John Murray Gibbon, the CPR's brilliant publicity agent, pitched a plethora of options as the "World's Greatest Travel System." The Oxford-educated former journalist's efforts in the Rockies were extensive and creative. In addition to promoting artists, photographers and the arts to wealthy travelers, he was instrumental in the forming outdoor groups beginning with the Trail Riders of the Canadian Rockies. Interest in trail riding was waning, and in 1923, Gibbon took the simple pack trip, gave it an elitist twist and created a "fraternity" of riders.

It seemed that anyone who put his fanny to a saddle wanted to be a Trail Rider. Two hundred and seven members went on the group's first ride in 1924, and by 1929, membership was over 1,500. To give the idea extra cachet, riders were supposed to "earn" their way into the club by acquiring buttons based on the miles traveled by horse along the mountain trails—the first button was for fifty miles.

Basil Gardom's one-year-old son, Garde, became the youngest trail-rider when his father, much to his mother's annoyance and nurse's consternation, took him from Chateau Lake Louise to Moraine Lake.

The Sky Line Trail Hikers and the Ski Runners of the Canadian Rockies would follow—created as clubs to encourage travel to the backcountry and bungalow camps.

While many guests began or ended their trips at the major hotels, the backcountry facilities were meant to assure the extended patronage of visitors to settings so breathtaking that artists, photographers, mountaineers, royalty and celebrities—along with the "ordinary man"—embraced the region with an equal sense of awe.

The "ordinary man's" changing tastes eroded the CPR's interest in backcountry and bungalow camps. The first car was allowed into the parks in 1911, and roads and highways that followed altered the face of the national parks. Bungalow camps along roadways catered to car travel, but soon, tourists opted for low-cost campgrounds over cabins. The Depression and World War II had tremendous impact on the

railway and its hotel and bungalow camp plans. Gradually, the railway sold off or simply abandoned its camps and tea houses.

*Bungalow camps built along the newly developed roadways and trails offered rustic "wilderness" accommodations for "dudes" seeking tamed adventure.*

Bungalow Camps in the Canadian Rockies

Canadian Pacific

*Left: The CPR tracks ran through the Bow Valley where Mount Rundle was more than a gorgeous vision. The Banff Springs Hotel that stands today was built of the mountain's stone.*

*Basil Gardom, astride his horse Cardinal in front of Chateau Lake Louise, was supervisor of construction and repairs for the CPR's western hotels. Gardom was instrumental in the development and construction of backcountry camps in the Rockies, and also supervised additions to Banff Springs Hotel, Chateau Lake Louise, the Empress Hotel, and construction of Crystal Gardens in Victoria.*

*While Gardom planned the mountain retreats, the CPR helped organize and promote groups like the Trail Riders of the Canadian Rockies.*

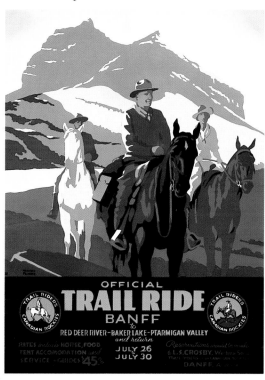

## The Legacy

The lodges featured within these pages are gems situated in astounding settings, and each has a story worth telling. The hotels, chalets, tea houses, bungalow camps and backcountry lodges of the Canadian Rockies cover an architec-tural, social, and economic spectrum found nowhere else.

These buildings reflect the growth of a country with strong parental ties to Europe and sibling rivalry with its neighbor to the south. The grand hotels are neither the castles of Europe nor the frontier log structures that grace Ameri-ca's national parks. The backcountry camps and cabins are as organic to their setting as the very forests from which they were built. The architectur-al roots may reach across the Atlantic and tap south of the border, but they each remain uniquely Canadian.

# Grand Resorts

They are the architectural landmarks of the Canadian Rockies. Grand resorts on the well trodden pathways blazed by the railways then followed by highways. Each reflects the changing times and tastes of the touring public.

*Chateau Lake Louise, Banff National Park*

William Cornelius Van Horne, Canadian Pacific Railway's domineering general manager, was not a man to miss an opportunity. By 1883, the main line of the CPR had gnashed its way to within a few miles of Kicking Horse Pass. With the work season closing, three railway employees, brothers William and Thomas McCardell and Franklin McCabe, decided to remain near Banff for the winter.

Motivated by rumors of hot springs, they built a raft and found a cave in which sulphur-laden water filled a pool near the otherwise bone-chilling Bow River. Van Horne soon heard of their find, and he visited the Bow Valley site. The rail tycoon recognized the tremendous tourist potential of hot springs in such a grand setting. Government officials were already interested in designating the site as a park reserve fashioned after the national parks in the United States. Van Horne jumped on the idea, and professed that development in the mountain valley had to be protected from mineral and timber exploitation. And also from three young men who were desperately trying to lay claim to and profit from their springs discovery.

Van Horne had been eyeing the scenery along the railway's mountain stretch of track, searching for the perfect site for a park reserve and a showpiece hotel. His initial selection was near Lac des Arcs, where he envisioned a hotel on an island. But Van Horne had seen the area blanketed with fresh snow, and the following spring, it was little more than a dust bowl. The hot springs region with views fanning out from the valley floor would prove to be an inspirational setting. Today, the Banff Springs Hotel, on a promontory overlooking the Spray and Bow rivers, is a National Historic Site and one of the country's architectural treasures. Instead of a fine hotel, a massive cement plant operates at Exshaw near Van Horne's original site.

William Pearce, the federal superintendent of mines for the Department of Interior, submitted an order to Parliament to make twenty-six square kilometers on the north slopes of Sulphur Mountain a park reserve. On November 28, 1885, the order was approved and Canada's park system was born. The Canadian Pacific Railway had the government's blessing to develop the region for tourism, and plans were well underway when Rocky Mountains Park was formally established in 1887.

While the Canadian government never signed over Banff's hot springs to the railway, they did give the CPR near *carte blanche* when it came to hotel development. London-trained architect Thomas C. Sorby had created the small chalet-inspired mountain dining stations along the line, but for a grand hotel, Van Horne turned to New York architect Bruce Price. Price had studied under noted American architect Henry Hobson Richardson, and he was already working on the railway's Windsor Sta-

**OPENED: JUNE 1888**
**BUILT BY: CANADIAN PACIFIC RAILWAY**
**ARCHITECTS: BRUCE PRICE (ORIGINAL); WALTER PAINTER (1914 TOWER);**
**J.W. ORROCK (1928 NORTH AND SOUTH WINGS); CARRUTHERS, MARSHALL**
**& ASSOCIATES (1990 CONFERENCE CENTRE); ROBERT LEBLOND (1995 SOLACE SPA)**

The hotel's interior was never meant to reflect one period or one country:

The Grapes Wine Bar, above, was once the Writing Room and still features original grapevine molding, pegged oak-plank flooring and flat paneling meant to replicate a Scottish castle.

The Strathcona Room, upper right, was named after Lord Strathcona, one of the company's first directors. Designed as a private dining room, it has a Norman Gothic style.

The introduction of Spanish decor in the Spanish Walk, right, offers a transition into the same motif found in the adjoining Alhambra Dining Room and foyer. The painting at the end of the Walk was done by William Cornelius Van Horne.

Mount Stephen Hall, far right, with its 15th century Gothic architecture, illustrates the museum quality of the hotel's interior. Named after Lord Mount Stephen, the first president of the CPR, it is the hotel's crown jewel.

*Bruce Price's hotel, circa 1912, followed his credo: "A truly picturesque effect can never be produced deliberately...It can only be had by adding part to part and without deliberate design or intent."*

tion in Montreal. Price's success in Banff and with Windsor Station (1888-89) would spur him on to prestigious jobs for the Canadian Pacific: Chateau Frontenac in Quebec City (1893), Place Vigor Station and Hotel (1898), and Granville Street Station in Vancouver (1898). Price, who was the father of social etiquette maven Emily Post, left a legacy of sweeping variety in his work, both in Canada and the United States.

Critics and patrons alike tried to label the original hotel design. It was compared to a Tudor hall and Swiss chalet. CPR publicists saw the Scottish roots of Banff (named after Banffshire, Scotland) in every detail. It was picturesque with steep hipped roofs, peaked dor-

mers, turrets, balconies and bay windows. But the varied roof line, dormers, chimneys, oriel windows and cedar-shingle and stone accents of the exterior also reflected the Shingle style of architecture popular in the country surrounding Price's New York home. That style was fully played out in the architect's design of Tuxedo Park, New York (1885-1890), a vacation community that influenced a young Frank Lloyd Wright, and Price's design of the Banff Springs Hotel.

Price himself saw his body of work as reflecting the setting and blending with the environment: "...a house is but part of a scene, and the more complete the scene, the more naturally the house is

adapted to its surrounds, the better it fits into the landscape, the better the result."

Van Horne, an artist and amateur architect, was delighted with the CPR's quarter-million-dollar investment. The only variation between the completed hotel and Price's 1886 sketch was the elimination of the central pyramidal roof and the addition of a pavilion. Van Horne's biographer explains that Van Horne discovered—during construction—that the plans had not been followed, "...and the builder had turned the hotel the wrong side about, giving the kitchen the finest outlook." The "million dollar view" would be enjoyed by the kitchen staff instead of paying guests. Van Horne sketched a rotunda pavilion to be added returning the premier view to the guests.

Park Superintendent George Stewart was also pleased. He wrote in his 1887 Interior Report, "The hotel is now about completed and is an ornament to the Park and a credit to the enterprising proprietors."

When opened in June 1888, the hotel featured over 100 bedrooms, parlors, dining rooms, smoking rooms, a reading room and, for gentlemen, a billiard room and bar. The heart of the five-story center was an octagonal rotunda with overhanging balconies.

In Banff, the Canadian Pacific wanted to take advantage of the "healing" waters of the hot springs bearing the hotel's name, and pipes were laid from the springs to the hotel. Pools opened the following summer, with a detached bath house with separate "compartments" for ladies and for gentlemen.

The opening season was a huge success with 1,503 registered guests. Stewart continued his boosterism: "The advantages of this hotel to the Park are fully recognized, and the excellent accommodation it affords in every respect never fails to call forth the admiration of all who visit it."

During the 1890s, visitors were periodically detoured from the Canadian Rockies, whether by the 1892 small pox outbreak or the financial crisis that followed. Superintendent Stewart noted a fall in visitors during 1896. Numbers were down, but those who could afford to visit stayed longer.

As the economy improved, in 1902 the railway earmarked a half-million dollars for hotel additions and furnishing. A new version of the west wing was added on the south side of the building. But it seemed that no number of new rooms could meet the demand, and the 1903 season had to be extended to accommodate guests.

While the CPR expanded, in his 1904-05 Interior Report, Superintendent Stewart continued to document the growth: "Not withstanding the large extensions made to the building in 1903, which included the addition of over 200 rooms, the management has since found it necessary to make arrangements for yet another large addition, the work of

CPR architect Walter Painter's rendering for the "new" hotel paid homage to the original Bruce Price design, but the Rundle rock construction put it in context with its mountain setting.

construction of which will be proceeded with during the coming winter. This latest addition is being built with a view of its being utilized throughout the winter."

An announcement of the 180-by-60-foot five-story addition appeared in the June 1902 edition of *The Railway and Shipping World*, noting that the architects were Hutchison & Wood, Montreal. But speculation is that Francis M. Rattenbury, who was then heading the CPR's Pacific architectural offices, and had designed or was designing additions for Mount Stephen House, Glacier House and Lake Louise Chalet, was in part responsible for the work.

By 1905, the controversial union of

the Canadian government and the Canadian Pacific Railway investment in tourism was a success. Drawn by the scenery, hot springs and a first class hotel, and enticed to the area through a highly successful promotional campaign, guests were arriving from around the world: South Africa, the Hague, Paris, Austria, England, Japan, the United States, Borneo, Hong Kong and Canada. More additions sprouted from other wings, and two six-story towers rose up. Records of this construction are scant, but guests were not.

"Banff Springs Hotel, although now of enormous proportions, is entirely inadequate to the number of its patrons, and the Canadian Pacific Railway

*Above: Tunnel Mountain Drive curves as it heads into town with Banff Springs Hotel below.*
*Foldout: The massive Banff Springs Hotel seems small when seen in the panorama of Banff National Park.*

*Kate Reed, wife of CPR hotel's manager-in-chief, decorated the early hotel. Red English tiles, rich paneling and period chandeliers hung from the coffered ceiling of the Reception Hall, circa 1915.*

Company finds itself again compelled for the third time to make another large addition to its already magnificent building," wrote Superintendent Stewart in 1906.

The new addition would be more than an expansion, rather the beginning of a new hotel. CPR officials commissioned Walter Painter, an American and chief architect for the railway, for the job. Painter's plans called for an eleven-story concrete center tower flanked by two wings. Gone would be the wood-shingled turrets and varied roof line of Price's original design. The hotel would reflect the scenery in a different way: its tower would be faced with local Mount Rundle limestone. Perhaps Painter was inspired by the peaks of nearby Castle Mountain or the dominating presence of Mount Rundle itself, but the final result gave it a look of rock-solid permanence.

The design has been called a "Scottish Baronial derivation of the chateau style." With Painter's stone addition, the CPR's desire to link the hotel to Scotland was fulfilled. The hotel featured flat dormers, circular arches and round-headed windows, characteristics incorporating the Canadian Chateau Style of federal buildings and railway stations and hotels across the country.

At the end of the 1911 season, work crews began dismantling the existing center portion of the hotel, with blasting and excavating continuing through the winter. In place of wooden frame and sheathing was state-of-the-art steel and concrete construction, which enabled the hotel to be built on a monumental scale. The new wing was of beam and girder type, with solid floor slabs, and hooped columns. The dining room was 150 by 75 feet and lighted by four large ridge skylights.

"Framing for the dormer openings in the steep pitched roof slopes presented something of a problem in the forms for the concrete, but otherwise the design of the superstructure was reasonably simple," a building magazine of the time reported. Two hoist towers, a carpenter shop, a stone-cutting yard and a concrete plant were all housed on the main axis of the tower next to the dining room. Gravel deliveries, once planned from Calgary, were erratic, and a gravel plant was built seven miles below the hotel.

Painter supervised the design and construction. When finished, the hotel cost $1,500,000, and Walter Painter had gained extensive experience in a building type he would become famous for. The new wing, to be part of the "Painter Tower," was used during the 1912 season. Each winter, construction began anew to complete the Painter Tower. When finished in 1914, it was the tallest building in Canada.

Guests still enjoyed the "great outdoors," but were searching for more attainable goals than conquering peaks. The first nine-hole golf course was built in 1911, and redesigned as an eighteen-hole course by Stanley Thompson in 1927.

The spa image of the hotel was enhanced with the $35,000, 1912 construction of two swimming pools and a bath house designed by Painter. Again, the building material was mass and reinforced concrete. A two-story bathhouse was topped by a promenade accessed from the hotel lobby. Turkish baths, massage rooms, steam room and drying rooms filled the top floor, with 100 dressing rooms on the ground level. An eighty-by-twenty-foot, partially enclosed hot sulphur pool was off the dressing rooms, and an arched loggia ran between the sulphur pool and the semi-circular fresh-water pool.

When guests arrived in May 1914, they found the luxurious new tower with 300 guest rooms, a dining room and rotunda, all exquisitely furnished and designed by Kate Reed, wife of CPR hotel's manager-in-chief Hayter Reed. Red English tiles and Persian rugs covered the main floors, rich wood paneling swathed the walls, period chandeliers hung from coffered ceilings and wicker furniture filled the rooms.

The completed expansion cost $2 million, but with the onset of World War I, only half the number of guests stayed at the hotel as had vacationed there the previous year.

During the next twelve years, major expansion was mothballed along with Painter's plans for the two new wings. A portion of the original wing that had served as kitchen and dining room was torn down, guest rooms were redecorated, and laundry and boiler room facilities were added. If the changes seemed mundane, the clientele did not.

Besides a steady stream of royalty, politicians, European aristocracy and American and Canadian guests flaunting their newfound wealth, the glamour of Hollywood descended on Banff. In 1920, *Conceit*, starring Hedda Hopper, Maurice Costello, Betty Hilburn and William Davidson was filmed in Banff. It was the first of a string of films to use the incredible beauty of the Canadian Rockies as a backdrop. Once again, it was time to expand.

Instead of bringing Painter back to finish his hotel, the CPR hired J.W. Orrock to design the two-wing addition. Painter had gone on to create an addition to Chateau Lake Louise, completed in 1913. He also designed the Cave and Basin bathing facilities in Banff that opened in 1914, and his own home along the Bow River in Banff. Painter left as CPR's chief architect to pursue his interest in ready-cut and sectional housing and precast concrete construction.

*Provincial crests are displayed in the carved beam molding of Mount Stephen Hall.*

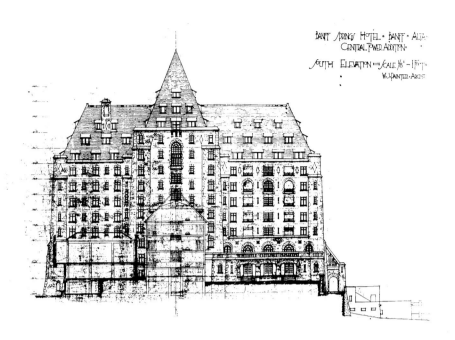

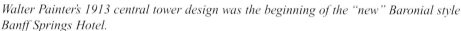

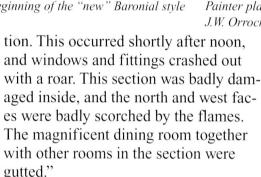

*Walter Painter's 1913 central tower design was the beginning of the "new" Baronial style Banff Springs Hotel.*

*Painter planned on adding two additions to his tower, but it was J.W. Orrock whose wing plans were completed in 1928.*

To house Banff Springs Hotel guests during construction, a Tudor-style, 100-bedroom annex was constructed and completed by March 1926. On April 6, 1926, plans for demolishing the original building became moot. At 11 a.m., the assistant manager and a CPR publicist noticed smoke rising from the north wing. A fire report was filed, but within an hour the hotel was ablaze. By 2 p.m., the original wing was a smoldering pile of rubbish.

The April 9th edition of *Crag & Canyon* reported: "Fire totally destroyed the north wing of the fine C.P.R. edifice on Wednesday, and damage in the central stone portion, completed in 1913, is considerable. All fixtures and furniture in the rooms on the outer face and the dining room being entirely burned...The spectacular blaze was added to by an explosion, supposedly from heat combustion, in the tower of the centre sec-

tion. This occurred shortly after noon, and windows and fittings crashed out with a roar. This section was badly damaged inside, and the north and west faces were badly scorched by the flames. The magnificent dining room together with other rooms in the section were gutted."

The newspaper also reported the CPR's plans to reopen the hotel by mid-July. Company president Sir Edward Beatty was on the scene, and he allocated $2 million for constructing new wings and restoring the fire-damaged tower. The hotel did indeed reopen July 1, 1926.

Orrock took Painter's concept and made it bigger—much bigger. Not only did Orrock increase the size of the wings, but also he expanded the Painter Tower and modified its roof-line. Still, Orrock treated Painter's plans with respect, finally uniting what had been a

style in transitional conflict. The two wings were set at an angle rather than the straight line Painter had envisioned, and the tower roof added more variety to the hotel's silhouette, putting it in comfortable context with its mountainous setting.

Basil Gardom, superintendent of construction and repairs for the CPR's western hotels, supervised the work. The north wing was framed in steel then enclosed in a wooden cocoon to shelter workers during winter construction. By the spring of 1927, the wooden shelter was removed and the completed wing, now faced in Rundle limestone, stood finished. The old south wing was demolished at the end of the 1926 season, and the new wing debuted seven months later in April 1928. All but the

*Right: The creation of the Solace Spa in 1995 brought back the days of Banff Springs Hotel as an elegant spa resort.*

*The restoration of the Oval Room, below, features ochre gold Venetian plastered walls and Czechoslovakian crystal chandeliers.*

*The adjoining 5,634-square-foot Cascade Ballroom has the original plaster beams and decorative scroll ceiling work with a contemporary bit of fluff in the new painted cloud motif, right.*

Tudor annex was finished with the exquisitely cut Mount Rundle stone. By the time it opened for the 1928 season, the railway had spent $9 million on the hotel, and in so doing, created a Canadian castle.

The hotel's castle motif was reinforced by meticulous interior design. Reproductions of Jacobean European furniture fill many of the Baronial-inspired great halls, anterooms, and colonnades. Suits of armor, coats of arms, and Medici prints enhance the European image. Yet details of Canadian and Native peoples' roots are not lost. Fanciful ornamental work includes depictions of Native figures, Canadian provincial crests, and local flora. Crockets—decorative hook-like spurs of stone carved in various leaf shapes and Indian figures—project at regular intervals from the angles of interior beams, balconies and doorways reinforcing the rooms' Gothic feel while reflecting their true setting.

Kate Reed, who had become the "grande dame of decoration" for many of the Canadian Pacific hotels, died in

1928, yet many feel her elegant influence (she had decorated the 1888 Banff Springs Hotel) was reflected in the "new" hotel. The Conservatory was filled with her signature wicker furniture. Michael Delahantry, former manager of the hotel, and Kate Treleaven, personal secretary to CPR president Sir Edward Beatty selected the furniture and artwork. The heavy wood furniture, replicas of European castle and manor pieces, was crafted by the Montreal company of Castle & Son Manufacturing.

The castle-like interior was never meant to be frozen in one time or one country. As it did in 1928, the hotel interior spans ages and geography.

Guests usually enter the hotel through the two-story Reception Hall. Paneled in red oak with heavy balustrades and glass-enclosed balconies, the space was first remodeled in 1902. Much of the original porch was later enclosed into the main lobby, and during the 1960s, the woodwork was painted an olive green. Recent restoration (replicating the 1911 version) restored the original wood paneling, and brought brass, glass and mirrors into the design in an attempt to lighten the space. Reproductions of the original chandeliers hang from the vaulted ceiling, but the hall is not indicative of the

museum-like glory of many of the other public rooms.

That glory is best experienced in the south wing's Mount Stephen Hall. Named after Lord Mount Stephen, the first president of the Canadian Pacific Railway, the great hall features 15th century Gothic architecture. The ceiling soars, and provincial coats of arms of

*A guest suite is appropriately decorated for the holidays.*

New Brunswick, Quebec, Manitoba, Prince Edward Island, Ontario, Saskatchewan, Nova Scotia, Alberta and British Columbia anchor each carved oak beam. It is a bit of a history lesson, since Newfoundland was not part of the confederation at the time. The floor is the irregular Bedford lime flagstone brought from Indiana.

The coat of arms of the Dominion of Canada is on one wall and the insignia of the Royal Canadian Mounted Police, official guardians of the national parks of Canada, on another. Crests of four presidents of the Canadian Pacific Railway shine like jewels in the towering leaded glass windows. Appointments include refectory tables and chairs, armor, Leonardo tapestries, and wrought-iron work that fronts the balconies and hangs as chandeliers from the ceiling.

The hotel features a number of exquisite private rooms including the Gothic Oak Room near the recessed spiral stairway. Next to it was the billiard room, now the Norquay Room.

A spiral stairway off the Oak Room to the mezzanine is an inspired transitional point. The stairway's treads, cut from fossilized Tyndall stone quarried from Manitoba, wrap around a crowned column. Tiffany sconces with thistle motifs gently illuminate the stairway. On the mezzanine level, guests can turn right and enter the foyer to the Alhambra Dining Room with its vaulted ceiling and bas relief of the *Santa Maria* above the fireplace. Hand-wrought bronze gates, valued when crafted at $30,000, lead to the Spanish-inspired dining room.

From the head of the stairway to the left is the Spanish Walk, a gallery bordered by wrought-iron railings, lighted by mica and wrought-iron lanterns and with a birdseye view of Mount Stephen Hall below.

A large and exquisite Writing Room once filled the space where the Grapes Wine Bar and hallway to the terrace now stand. The Writing Room was converted to retail space, then in 1984 when the terrace was added, the room was divided into the current Grapes Wine Bar and terrace entryway. The grape design in the crown molding and the wood paneling is original—hence the name of the bar—and the leaded and stained glass windows are also original. One of those windows was moved and used to divide the bar from the hallway. The bar, though hand-carved, is not original. Visitors still find stoic-faced Indians carved in the archways, and a perfect view through leaded glass windows.

One of the best loved rooms in the north wing's upper level is the River-view Lounge. Guests continue to position themselves in front of one of the eight arched Czechoslovakian-glass windows to take in the "million dollar view": the Bow River flowing northeast toward the distant peaks of the Fairholme Range and framed by the nearby cliffs of Tunnel Mountain on the left and Mount Rundle on the right. The room features a tunnel vaulted ceiling and is anchored by a massive Tyndall

stone fireplace featuring two carved ram's heads.

Another restoration of the hotel began in 1997 with the $8 million facelift of the Oval Room, Cascade Ballroom and Conservatory under the design direction of Kerry Busby of Calgary. The ochre gold Oval Room wall treatment is hand-done Venetian plaster that creates a rich silky feel. Czechoslovakian crystal chandeliers (moved from Toronto's Royal York Hotel in the 1970s) hang from the ceiling. At one time, a library was tucked between the stairway and the Oval Room. The richly paneled room still exists, but is now used for storage.

The Cascade Ballroom is entered through double doorways adorned by arched plaster moldings of fruits, flowers and nuts. The elegant plaster work is not original, but a hand-crafted addition of the current restoration. The ballroom is grander than the original in its appointments, with the addition of elaborate window treatments that were created, in part, to accommodate the needs of conventions. The plaster detailing, carved beams, panels and wall sconces are original, and the seafoam green walls are close to the first color. But look up, and a new touch of frivolity is found in the cloud motif painted on the ceiling. The chandeliers in the ballroom are from the Palliser Hotel in Calgary.

The once-wicker-filled Conservatory wraps around the end of the Cascade Ballroom. Restoration began by repairing

Ram's heads are carved in the Riverview Lounge Tyndall stone fireplace, right.

Heritage guest rooms, lower right, have been restored to the period with plaster molding and crystal chandeliers.

The crown pillar rises in the stairway axis, lower left, to the Alhambra Dining Room foyer.

Hand-wrought bronze gates open to the dining room, left.

the original trellis work, all hand painted in the French tradition. The wicker furniture is long gone, and the fountain was removed in the late 1980s, when the marble cracked. The room is rarely used for lounging guests as in the past, but for receptions and conventions.

The north wing's Garden Terrace Lounge was replaced by the Rob Roy Dining Room in 1972. But over the years, the Painter Tower and north and south wings have retained much of the remarkable grandeur that greeted guests in 1928.

That year, the Canadian Pacific Railway and the Banff Springs Hotel were ready for the season. They were not ready for the Great Depression that devastated both the Canadian and the United States economies, and drained revenues of the Canadian Pacific Railway and its properties.

Nothing bounces back like money. The years prior to World War II marked a grand time at the grand hotel. During the 1930s, a cosmopolitan array of guests and their entourages arrived for long summer holidays. Evenings included dancing to the hotel's own orchestra and enjoying concerts and lectures in Mount Stephen Hall. During the day, golf, tennis, trail riding, fishing, climbing or enjoying the hotel's pool were all entertainment options. The CPR sponsored The Highland Gathering and Music Festival beginning in 1927, and the once small-town Banff Indian Days became a grand western celebration.

World War II followed, and when the country finally recovered, the world was a very different place. Travel was no longer an indulgence of the rich, but an option for the middle class. Air travel replaced long distance train and ship travel, and the automobile made North American destinations, once only for the privileged, an economical adventure. The railway's mountain hotels fell into disrepair, and there was talk of tearing them down.

The grand hotels struggled to find a market, then in 1969, the CPR opened the Banff Springs Hotel to winter guests, targeting skiers. Under the management of Ivor Petrak (who was also the general manager of Chateau Lake Louise) and design direction of Laszlo Funtek, consultant from the Banff Centre for the Arts who worked on the hotel's interior design from 1972 into the late 1990s, the hotel was renovated room by room. In search of new markets and new space, the exterior balconies and terraces were enclosed in glass, creating modern-day obtrusions in the stone facade. The half-circle fresh-water swimming pool was replaced by a small rectangular pool.

From 1965 to 1975, Funtek transformed staff rooms, storage, mechanical and elevator areas into sixty-seven additional guest rooms and some of the hotel's premier suites. The three-story Presidential Suite with its marble entrance, private elevator, lap pool, tapestry-shrouded master bedroom, sunken

living room with wood-burning fireplace and balcony/library were once mundane quarters for staff and storage. Not only are the views of the Bow River, Tunnel and Rundel mountains luscious, but for architectural buffs, it is an opportunity to admire the exterior stonework, turrets and roof lines.

Many of the architect's exterior towers, turrets and bridgeways are cocoons for accommodations. For example, an eight-sided Heritage Premium room with molded ceiling is charming in every detail. And while many of the rooms are successful makeovers, a few border on the bizarre—most notably a center room with a small kitchen and bedroom, tiny windows, and an elegant double stairway leading up to the bathroom.

The Vice Regal section of the hotel was renovated for Queen Elizabeth's visit in 1959. The tiled foyer is done in a monastery style, dimly lighted and reminiscent of the Spanish Walk. Ten individual rooms are accessed off the foyer. Each room has its own charm with oak detailing, wainscoting and ceiling molding.

Expansion of the hotel began anew in 1987 to help meet the anticipated needs of the 1988 Winter Olympic Games. The Tudor annex was renovated into guest rooms and renamed Manor Wing. Petrak retired in 1991, and Edward Kissane took over management reins under the new Canadian Pacific Hotels and Resorts banner.

One hundred million dollars was allocated towards the long-range restoration and renovation of the hotel. In November 1990, the $25 million Conference Centre, designed by Carruthers, Marshall & Associates of Calgary, opened to accommodate the growing convention traffic. The exterior—linked to the Manor Wing by an arched walkway—is covered with two million pounds of Mount Rundle stone. The Centre's varied roofline, with gables and turrets, blends with that of the original hotel. The 150,000-square-foot addition features a ballroom, audiovisual theatre, meeting rooms, business centre, five pin bowling facility, and twenty-nine suites with a separate reception lobby. A statue of William Cornelius Van Horne stands in the courtyard.

The design and decor of the new wing reflects the hotel's Scottish Baronial style. Calgary interior designer Kerry Busby took some of the organic elements of the Scottish look, like the thistle motif of the main hotel, and merged them with English Arts & Crafts colors and patterns. Carpets and wall coverings were selected based on William Morris period designs. The huge buffalo head trophies that once graced the Reception Hall were moved to the new Manor Lobby.

The Banff Springs Hotel's connection to the original hot springs was dammed by the removal of the "healing" sulphur waters from the hotel pool in 1926, and the later destruction of the semi-circular swimming pool. Nearly a century after

*Wicker furniture once filled the Conservatory, and the original fountain, shipped from New York, was removed after it cracked. But the beautifully restored lattice work illustrates the Conservatory's historic garden-room roots.*

the original hot springs were discovered, the spa resort business again flourished. In 1995, the $12 million, 35,000-square-foot Solace Spa opened at the hotel. Designed by Robert LeBlond of Calgary, the Solace is a contemporary interpretation of the original Banff Springs hot springs and pool complex.

The graceful Rundle rock loggia still stands along the indoor cold-water swimming pool. The addition of the Solace Spa complex between the Reception Hall and original swimming pool is a seamless step through time. LeBlond created an entry that invites and embraces visitors. This may be an addition, but the past trickles through each level as unobtrusively as the water falling into the soaking pools.

Rundle rock columns support the domed skylight of the salt-water mineral pool. An interpretive mosaic of Rocky Mountain wildflowers is set into the pool's floor. Three massage pools—each with a cascading waterfall and of a different temperature—surround the mineral pool.

LeBlond's inspiration for the soft contour of the Solace Spa came from the curved and arched ceilings of the Alhambra Dining Room foyer. The architect took the feminine lines of the foyer from the otherwise Baronial and masculine hotel and transposed them to a spa "that celebrates the human body." The architect also borrowed the textured faux finish of Mount Stephen's Hall and the Riverview Lounge for interior spa walls, and bas

*Banff Springs Hotel and Banff townsite as seen from Sulphur Mountain.*

relief peacock-design water fountains were salvaged from the hotel and moved to the spa and pool area. Curved glass around the sunroom and workout and aerobics area are detailed in the same fashion as the original Conservatory off the Cascade Ballroom. And as was the original intent, promenades top the rooflines merging the grand outdoors with interior spaces.

Men's and women's steam rooms, saunas, inhalation rooms, whirlpools, lounges, treatment rooms and sun terraces have replaced the old dressing rooms and Turkish baths. There are also indoor and outdoor whirlpools.

William Cornelius Van Horne would be impressed.

If the spa would impress Van Horne, the current restoration of the 1928 Banff Springs Hotel now underway must be creating quite a stir with the spirits of Bruce Price, Walter Painter, J.W. Orrock, Kate Reed and others who dreamt of and created this Canadian castle.

The courtyard entrance into the Reception Hall can no longer accommodate the flood of guests. In 1999, a major expansion and upgrade of the Spray Avenue arcade level entrance, designed by Robert LeBlond, began. A thirty-foot addition, faced in Rundle rock, will be added, and check-in desks and offices will be moved to the new facility. Besides providing easier access to the hotel, the change gives the old

Reception Hall a new lease on life. It will be restored as a great hall, and windows will open up Van Horne's "million dollar views." As LeBlond notes, "The goal is to pick up the spirit of Banff, to enhance and respect what is there. Every project is supposed to contain the spirit of the hotel."

*An array of flags waves above the hotel entrance.*

Who can more easily capture that spirit than a child? A young boy rushes down a hallway. His black cape swirls behind him; his sister, in a royal blue baroque gown, runs to keep up. "Are they in a pageant?" someone asks their mother, dressed in 1990s black leather. "It is his dream," she answers. "His

dream—to be in a castle."

"Yes, my dream," the boy repeats with a serious gaze. "My dream," he says again as the youngster prances through the Gothic wonderland.

Of course, the Banff Springs Hotel has always been a dream—that is the spirit of the place. That children can still find magic careening through archways, up corkscrew stairways, past convention stations, and shops, and simply see the wonder in their wake is a testament to the ability of the young to ignore what doesn't fit that "dream" and find what does.

That is the key to the hotel, to look beyond shopping arcades, conventioneers with name tags and bustle of bellmen to find the true treasures. Those treasures begin with its setting in Canada's first national park. It is a place that reflects another time, a time long before William Cornelius Van Horne decided a luxury hotel would be a huge economic boon to the Canadian Pacific Railway. Long before New York architect Bruce Price began plans for the first chateau-style hotel with a "million dollar view." Long before one man's dream was burned or dismantled, and another man's constructed with chunks of blue-gray Mount Rundle limestone.

The Banff Springs Hotel is a place where children can still play dress-up and make their own dreams come true.

*Chateau Lake Louise began as a tiny wooden chalet on the shores of one of Canada's natural treasures. It has evolved into a sprawling and elegant destination resort.*

Minerals and silt from massive glaciers have trickled over time into the 273-foot-deep crevice that is Lake Louise. Tiny bits of pigment settle in the depths of what seems like the center of the earth and return a stunning shade of blue-green. Even today, with thousands of tourists drawn to the shoreline to see the image captured in countless advertising campaigns, it is a gem, a diamond set squarely in the rough and tumble wonders of the Rocky Mountains.

The beauty and almost mystical powers of Lake Louise were first described by the Stoney Indians to railway surveyors. Tom Wilson, an assistant to the chief Canadian Pacific Railway surveyor Major A.B. Rogers, is reputed to be the first white man to have seen the lake in 1882. "Lake of Little Fishes," as the Indians named it, was rechristened in 1884 to honor Princess Louise Caroline Alberta, daughter of Queen Victoria.

Railway men cut a path from their Laggan station to the lake, and artists and alpinists shared in its glory. CPR president William Van Horne saw the tourist potential in the mountains west of Banff, and ordered construction of a small Swiss Alps chalet at the lake.

The elegant chateau of concrete, glass and steel that hugs the shores of Lake Louise gives no hint of its humble beginnings. A simple thirty-five-by-fifty-foot frame Chalet Lake Louise opened in 1890 to meet the basic needs of those in search of adventure. Those guests

had little interest in the comforts of a grand hotel, but desired the challenge of blazing trails and conquering peaks. They would live and die in those crags and crevasses, their impressions and adventures documented in journals and guidebooks.

"Lake Louise has the enduring attraction of nature in one of her grandest and most inspiring moods...Lake Louise is a realisation of the perfect beauty of nature beyond the power of imagination."
—Walter Wilcox,
*The Rockies of Canada*, 1900

What writers couldn't capture, artists and photographers did, and Lake Louise was destined to become an icon of the Canadian Rockies.

Just as guests were discovering the quaint chalet, on June 19, 1893, it burned to the ground leaving the charred chimney as a lone sentinel on the shoreline. With railway efficiency, the CPR decided within days to replace the building. By July 3, engineer D.A. Stewart had plans for a chalet, "clap-boarded or shingled on the outside and sheeted inside would be about $2500." It was a simple square building with a single dormer, a bank of windows and verandah spanning the front. Accommodations were seven bedrooms and a reception room that also served as a dining room. The railway reaped the benefits of keeping tourists in the region, and the following year, the CPR decided to "...make Lake Louise a place of interest" to draw guests when they left the Banff Springs Hotel. These guests took the train to Laggan station

**OPENED: 1890 ∼ BUILT BY: CANADIAN PACIFIC RAILWAY**
**ARCHITECTS: CPR STAFF ARCHITECT (ORIGINAL &1893 REPLACEMENT, BURNED);**
**THOMAS SORBY (1898-99 ADDITIONS, DISMANTLED); FRANCIS M. RATTENBURY (1902 ADDITION, BURNED);**
**WALTER PAINTER (1906 ADDITION, BURNED, AND 1912 PAINTER WING);**
**BAROTT AND BLACKADER (1925 BAROTT WING); CARRUTHERS, MARSHALL & ASSOCIATES (1986-90 GLACIER WING)**

and walked or rode by wagon three and a half miles to the chalet.

By 1896, CPR General Superintendent D.W. Whyte recommended a laundry list of improvements for the Laggan station and chalet including road grading, the addition of a boathouse, bridge, stables, and "... a few bedrooms to be erected as an annex to the chalet," although by spring Whyte feared an additional building would "disfigure the original structure."

"Disfigure" may have been too strong a term for the first expansion, but over time Chateau Lake Louise survived a structural puberty of sorts, an awkward meshing of styles that created growing pains with each disjointed addition.

In 1898, the chalet sprouted a second story and new roof-line, and the following year two rather no-nonsense wings designed by Thomas Sorby extended from it. Francis M. Rattenbury added a delightfully elaborate, shingled, Arts & Crafts-style, four-story wing in 1902. Two polygonal towers capped by "candle-snuffer" roofs and a broad verandah with a jigsaw, snowflake-design balustrade added frivolity. (Rattenbury also designed large, elaborate additions to Sorby's Glacier House and Mount Stephen House in the Rockies and the first Hotel Vancouver.)

But additional space was needed, and Walter Painter, then chief architect for the CPR, replaced the Sorby wing and added a large seven-story structure in 1906. His style of choice was English Tudor Revival, popular in national parks buildings, featuring steeply pitched roofs, dormers and plaster and wood exterior. In an attempt to meld the Rattenbury Wing to the addition, Painter refaced the upper floor with plaster and wood then added what appear (from historic photographs) to be stone facades on the turrets.

Wildflowers and Icelandic poppies grew between the swampy lake shore and the chalet, and while the building was much larger, the chalet retained its intimacy and charm. The interior design was accomplished by Kate Reed, wife of manager-in-chief of CPR hotels Hayter Reed. She filled the hotel with Arts & Crafts style oak furniture, light fixtures and Persian rugs, and her work for CPR hotels became legendary.

Those alterations were child's play compared to the 1912 addition of the Painter Wing. The chalet housed 12,459 guests during the 1911 summer season, and Hayter Reed wrote CPR president Sir Thomas Shaughnessy that "...60 persons arrive daily at the chalet and cannot be accommodated" with as many as eight people to a room and cots "placed in every conceivable place as well as the drawing room."

Work crews, under Painter's supervision, had begun expansion at Banff Springs Hotel, and Reed suggested that those crews also work at Lake Louise. Shaughnessy authorized the plans for expansion in August 1911, then a month later instructed that three cottages be built while the extension was under construction. Painter's Montreal-based CPR offices designed Lakeside, Fairview and Hillside cottages. They resembled country homes with low pitched hipped roofs, dormers and exposed rafters, two reflecting the Tudor style of Painter's addition and the third the Shingle style more in keeping with the Rattenbury wing.

But it was the Painter extension that forever changed Lake Louise's character. Made of concrete and steel, flat-roofed and flat-faced, the stuccoed addition was reminiscent of an Italian villa with a large hexagonal tower serving as the entrance at one end, and a smaller square tower at the other. An elegant arched loggia along the lakeside ground level was the only ornamentation except for a few decorative balconies. While the addition introduced a grand hotel to the lake, the sight of it jarred most everyone who first saw it.

Painter was not relying on the past success of the chalet or chateau design that was defining Canadian mountain architecture to the traveling public. He saw himself as a contemporary architect, and his addition reflected that. Perhaps the design was Painter's interpretation of "organic architecture." Instead of looking to the forested landscape, jutting rocky peaks and incredibly blue water in front of the hotel, Painter's concrete whiteness seems to mirror massive Victoria Glacier. If Banff Springs Hotel was called the "snow castle," the Painter

A narrow gauge rail line carried guests from the new station to the chalet, now featuring Walter Painter's 1906 English Tudor Revival addition.

Wing may have been the "ice fortress."

In truth, one word drove the design: fire. Even in the planning stages, the 1912 addition was dubbed "the fire-proof wing." Fire was a harsh reality for both the parks and the railway. Flames had swept through the original Lake Louise Chalet in 1893, and during the 1920s, would reduce part of Banff Springs Hotel and wooden portions of Chateau Lake Louise to ashes.

Still, once visitors stepped inside the new wing, they saw the other side of the Painter design, one that embraced them in a contemporary sense of luxury—as the *nouveaux riches* of Canada and the U.S. expected. By then, the hotel's name was the more appropriate Chateau Lake Louise.

"The atmosphere of the Chateau is spaciousness. One is met at the entrance of the rotunda by a great open fire with the burning logs crackling a warm welcome. The most notable feature of the Chateau is perhaps the new wing...constructed of concrete. The whole of the ground floor is the spacious dining-room. Great windows looking out up the lake and hung with flower-boxes rich with trailing ferns, make this one of the most splendid dining-rooms that could be imagined outside of an artist's dream. Above it are four bedroom floors. The ball-room, formerly the dining-room, is in the old building, It is beautifully decorated in strawberry and rose color."

*Canadian Pacific*, Montreal, April 1, 1919

Instead of arriving at the revamped hotel by wagon, guests used a narrow gauge rail line between the station (constructed in 1910) and chalet. The strength of guests, who were intent on climbing the surrounding peaks, was preserved, and they were pulled in gasoline powered tram cars up the hill to the chalet at 5,670 feet.

The grounds were also transformed, and the fields of wild flowers and stone walls were replaced by formal lawns and paved pathways. A concrete retaining wall and landfill transposed the swampy lake access. This wave of CPR construction took place just as the Parks Branch of the Canadian government was created, and land use issues flared up. Eventually, a compromise was reached and building continued.

In 1915, F.L. Hutchinson, who had replaced Hayter Reed as manager-in-chief of CPR hotels, requested $148,222.70 to build a new kitchen, expand the dining room and make other alterations to the increasingly popular chalet. The two-floor expansion plans were submitted by Messrs. Barott, Blackader & Webster, who would later influence the face of the hotel on Lake Louise. The request was granted within months. Shaughnessy saw the economic logic in Hutchinson's assertion that "these improvements would not only comfortably take care of all its guests but be a powerful inducement to make them prolong and periodically renew their visits." Or perhaps he was concerned with the drop in guests from 12,826 in 1913 to only 8,280 in 1914, as recorded in an Interior Department Report.

Then on July 3, 1924, almost predictably, disaster struck:

"Chalet Lake Louise Hotel on fire and am advised beyond control Will get further particulars quickly as possible."—*2:38 p.m., C. Murphy*

"North Wing…now reported to be all gone and fire under control. The phone from station to hotel is out of commission. hard to get any information. They are getting engines moving to render any assistance possible. Will let you know as soon as can get further particulars."—*2:48 p.m., Winnipeg, Man. July 3rd*

"Two fire trucks and engines have been rushed from Banff over the highway to assist with fire. They left few minutes ago. Expect to be able to make there by hour and half. They can make much faster going by road than to load them on cars. over railway, would take too long load and unload.

"Fire started in cooks quarters near as they can tell it has burned north wing completely and is now burning over in the rotunda and still out of control. The first advise we got was at 12:40."—*W.D. Winnipeg 3:05 p.m.*

"Expect save new wing, last report just received says, but the old part however all caved in. That's up to the minute."—*W.D. Winnipeg July 3 3:40 p.m.*

"They expect take care of passengers off No. 7 and 8 which indicates they have it in hand."—*W.D. Winnipeg July 3. 3:53 p.m.*

"Old wing gone, new wing can be saved. No assistance from Calgary will be of any use by the time it reaches Lake Louise, part of the wooden building between rotunda and the new wing is now fairly drenched with water.

"Satisfied that the assistance of Banff fire brigade will be able to save new building. Wires all burned down.

"Personal effects of guests have been taken out.

"One or two of staff hurt in fighting fire, but not seriously."—*Phoned by Mr. J. McMillan to Mr. Usher, 4:05 p.m., July 3, 1924*

The hodgepodge of wooden additions was gone. But the Painter Wing had indeed proved "fireproof." The day after the disaster, CPR officials discussed the replacement building, and the Montreal firm of Barott and Blackader was selected to prepare plans.

Since 1911, the Parks Branch, consolidated and headquartered in Ottawa, had an interest in CPR hotel construction. Lake Louise was now part of Rocky Mountains Park (later renamed Banff National Park), and Commissioner of Dominion Parks James B. Harkin rejected Barott's first drawings. "I have never admired the newer portion of the Chateau (by Painter) and it seems to me that the proposed extension will be even less attractive," he wrote to CPR's A.O. Seymour.

*Guests seem rather bored as they watch the spectacle of the 1924 fire that destroyed the wooden portion of Chalet Lake Louise. More concrete was to come.*

*The just-completed fireproof Painter Wing was a jarring juxtaposition to the remodeled and already expanded Chalet, circa 1913.*

The concrete addition was slightly amended with a nod towards the chateau style favored by Harkin. It was Harkin who later persuaded the federal government to establish an advisory board for historic site preservation.

The nine-story building was made of reinforced concrete around a steel frame. Brick, stone and stucco walls, tile floors, and a near faceless front gave it an institutional look broken only by a series of dormers lined up against the slightly sloping roof like a row of tin soldiers standing watch over the remarkable panorama. An additional octagonal tower anchored the face of concrete punctuated by dozens of identical windows. Two stories of bedrooms were installed over a portion of the existing Painter Wing.

During the renovation, Painter's original rotunda (now to be the center tower) was reconfigured, transforming the pivotal Italianate tower into Barott's blocky version. The 1998 Heritage Character Statement confines that designation to the Painter Wing: "The 1924-25 addition is not considered to be a particularly fine example of the Chateau Style and overshadows some of the earlier Italianate features such as the central tower."

While critics of the design were vocal, no one criticized the remarkable task of constructing the hotel addition that opened the following June.

The passenger trams of the narrow gauge were converted to freight trucks, and twenty-eight tons of building material inched up the winding three-and-a-half-mile track to the site. Ironically, Basil Gardom, whose first job with the CPR had been driving the passenger tram from the rail station to the chateau, oversaw the construction in his capacity as supervisor of construction and repairs for the railway's western hotels.

The steel frame was encased in a wooden "hoarding" five feet away from the building so workers could proceed with the concrete during sub-zero days. The ground floor slab was poured before freezing and the second to eighth floors completed in seventeen days. By the week before Christmas, the top floor had been poured.

When finished, the addition—at a cost of nearly $2 million—featured approximately 288 guest rooms, a thirty-eight-by-eighty-foot rotunda, lake view lounge, ballroom with its own lounge, offices and curio shops on the main floor and a tavern, billiard room, ladies' hairdressing parlor, photographer's darkroom and service and storage areas on the lower floor. Decorated in mauve and rose, it was the place to see and be seen.

A swimming pool, designed by P.L. James, who had worked with Rattenbury and the CPR on a number of projects, became another symbol of the chateau. Dressing rooms were terraced into the hillside in front of the Painter Wing, and a graceful arched loggia surrounded the pool. Formal gardens and lawns were landscaped, and a putting green was added to what had once been a tiny chalet on the swampy fringes of the still stunning setting.

The Canadian Pacific advertised it as the "largest and most modern equipped chateau in the world." Staffed by 425 men and women with three managers to oversee operations, Lake Louise was ready for a new era.

That new era was strongly reflected in the bold unsentimental architecture of Chateau Lake Louise. The concrete combination of Painter's Italianate villa and Barott's faintly chateau-like addition was a stark departure from the railway's and Canadian government's "Canadian Chateau" design and the Tudor Revival architecture embraced by the National Parks Branch.

The distinctive image of Chateau

Hand maiden figurines in the chandeliers, left, replicate the originals now in the Edelweiss foyer. Hand sculpted and cast, the new figurines hold torches in honor of the 1988 Winter Olympic Games.

The old lobby, foreground, is now a lounge and graceful transition into the new Entry Pavilion, background. With its curved double stairway, rich woodwork and arches, the Pavilion reflects the styles of the Painter and Barrott wings.

Lake Louise is framed in the Venetian window of the Lobby Bar. Originally heavily draped, now delicate decorative painting emphasizes the European mountain chateau motif.

Lake Louise was unlike anything in the national parks properties, and if it had an underlying image, it was that of exclusivity. As one regular guest described it: "...The Chateau was rather forbidding in its exterior aspect, but the interior was spacious and charming with great plate glass windows in the lounge...onto that marvelous vista of lake and mountains. It was a friendly place, too—not overcrowded and more like a big country club than a hotel."

Hollywood descended on Lake Louise and the cast and crews of films like *Enticement* (1924) with Mary Astor and *Eternal Love* (1928), starring John Barrymore, entertained staff and guests.

But the real stars who frequented the chateau were the regulars who returned each season to climb another peak.

Those glamorous "clubby" days of the chateau were changing. A road between Banff and Lake Louise opened in 1921, and day trippers began frequenting Lake Louise. The Parks Branch surveyed three blocks of villa lots along the lake and opened them for lease that year. Suddenly, low-cost rooms, souvenir stands and restaurants sprouted. Next to the elegant Chateau Lake Louise, a log structure was built in 1922 by Louis and Gertrude Crosby. The Lake Louise Trading Company would eventually become Deer Lodge, a sprawling mélange of at least four distinct structures that were built, converted and redesigned over time.

As the highway system evolved, the Parks Branch encouraged the construction of camps along roadways like Paradise Bungalow Camp (1935-1940) built following plans of the Architecture and Town Planning Division of the National Parks Service in Ottawa. Lake Louise Ski Lodge and cabins (later called Post Hotel) opened in 1942.

Chateau Lake Louise, along with the Banff Springs Hotel, closed during World War II. When it reopened, the chateau was far from grand. It had suffered from neglect, and the tastes of the traveling public had changed, resulting in dreadfully low revenues. There was talk of demolishing the concrete giant.

The Trans Canada Highway was

(AA) SECTION THROUGH ELEVATOR HALL   (D-D) SECTION THROUGH BALL ROOM & STAIRWAY   END ELEVATION

*Barrott and Blackader submitted blueprints in September 1924 that show the proposed ballroom and stairway of the Chateau Lake Louise. The Italianate elements of Painter's Wing were replaced by a subdued chateau style usually identified with railway hotels pre-1920.*

*Decorative painting and new windows are the only noticeable changes in the restored Victoria Dining Room, part of the 1912 Painter Wing.*

*Swiss Alps traditions live on the edge of Lake Louise, above.*
*Sleigh rides are a popular way to view the area when the lake freezes and snow shrouds the landscape, below.*

completed in 1957 through the park, and in 1959 and 1960 three ski runs were created on Whitehorn Mountain across the valley. Lake Louise was becoming a year round resort.

The chateau briefly opened for the winter in 1975. Swiss guide Edward Feuz, then in his nineties, was brought up from his home in Golden to formally unlock the winter gate. During the ceremony, the hotel manager instructed Feuz to "throw away the key," which he promptly pitched into the woods. It was soon chillingly evident that the chateau was not ready for winter habitation, and it closed.

In 1982, after the necessary renova-tions, the chateau again opened for the winter season. This time the hotel was ready to shield guests from the notori-ously bone-chilling elements.

In anticipation of crowds and revenue generated by the 1988 Winter Olympic Games, major renovation was slated. Between 1986 and 1990, Canadian Pacific Hotels and Resorts invested $65 million on expansion and restoration. Besides the structural improvements, Ivor Petrak (who managed Banff Springs Hotel and directed all mountain hotel operations) and designer Laszlo Funtek (who was also a design consult-ant at Banff Springs Hotel) decided that the interior should have the feel of a European hunting lodge. Chateau Lake Louise's history, so strongly linked to the Swiss guides hired by the CPR beginning in 1899, would reflect those European mountain roots.

It is that alpine flavor that fills Cha-teau Lake Louise.

The European motif has been carried out almost seamlessly through each addition. In 1988, the Glacier Wing, designed by Carruthers, Marshall & As-sociates of Calgary, was completed. What was once the circular drive is now the stunning two-story Entry Pavilion. This rotunda emits the same elegance that the earlier chateau's reputation was built on. The expansion also added 150 guest rooms, the Edelweiss Dining Room, a shopping arcade, the Walliser Stube Wine Bar and 400-car parking arcade.

Gone are the dull brown, rust and navy tones of the 1960s. Instead, the original strawberry, rose and heritage green dominate the color scheme.

The Edelweiss entry hall and part of the dining room now fill the space that was once the grand ballroom and lounge. The ballroom had already been converted to the Fairview Dining Room as guests lost interest in waltzing away the evening, and the hotel sought badly needed dining space.

Designer Kerry Busby of Calgary embraced Funtek's alpine chalet interior design concept and researched the Bavarian region of Europe for inspiration. Some of that inspiration was found a bit closer to home.

The antique "hand maiden" chandeliers hanging in the Edelweiss entry hall once hung from the entrance to the Rimrock Room of Calgary's Palliser Hotel. The maidens are dressed in European court costumes and mounted on Scottish stag antlers (as described in a 1960 postcard), and these originals were the basis for the other maiden chandeliers in the new rotunda and renovated lounge. The lovely ladies were hand-crafted in Calgary just prior to the Winter Olympics, so they are holding torches rather than antlers. The vintage ballroom chandeliers now hang along the lake side of

the Lakeview Lounge. The bird-cage shaped light fixtures along the hallway are also original.

Substantial Austrian Biedermeier furniture crafted in Calgary now fills the grand Entry Pavilion and original lounge. In contrast to the heavy mahogany furniture is the delicate hand-paint-

*The richly appointed Edelwiess Dining Room fills the space once devoted to a ballroom.*

ing gracing archways and beams of the imposing rooms. Montreal artist Holde Unverzagt did the painting, much of it featuring Alberta's provincial flower, the wild rose. The elegant arched windows were once draped, but now give an unobstructed view of Lake Louise. Lakeview Lounge's original quarry tile floors are carpeted up to the ten-foot-wide Tyndall stone stairway that rises to the Victoria Dining Room and its foyer.

The dining room looks much as in 1920-vintage photographs, including placement of its linen dressed tables. Bavarian painting now decorates the beams, but the chandeliers are restored originals. The Red Lounge foyer is at the top of the stairway, and a private dining room is behind the river rock and Tyndall stone fireplace wall of the Victoria Dining Room. All the attention to detail can almost be missed— the view is beyond description.

Guest rooms and suites have been restored in stages and reflect varying interpretations of the mountain motif. The Swiss Rooms were created in 1988. The blond Swiss-made furniture was moved from the Banff Springs Hotel and handmade paneling was added to the walls and ceiling.

Chateau Lake Louise is one of Canada's premier summer and winter resorts. It is both elegant and sturdy, facing off over blue-green waters with Mount Victoria.

*Since its beginning, Jasper Park Lodge has always been captured in the mirror reflection of Lac Beauvert.*

The towering Rundle-rock Banff Springs Hotel or elegant Chateau Lake Louise might both have fit as easily in cosmopolitan skylines of the era as they did set amidst the splendor of Banff National Park. But 180 miles north of Banff townsite, where icefields and milky blue glaciers introduce a devastatingly beautiful vista, the vintage Jasper Park Lodge and sophisticated bungalow camp could have been at home only in the mountains.

When the Canadian Pacific Railway abandoned the northerly route over Yellowhead Pass in preference to the Bow Valley corridor across the Rocky Mountains, the upper stretches of the peaks got a reprieve from development.

It wasn't until the Grand Trunk Pacific and Canadian Northern railways began laying tracks through the upper reaches of the Rockies, that interest rekindled in what is now Jasper National Park. In 1907, 5,000 square miles, including land through the Athabasca Valley and along the planned rail line, was designated a federal reserve in much the same manner as the Rocky Mountains Park had been in 1887. And as with its

counterpart to the south, railway executives were eyeing the wild wonderland along their lines for tourism.

The GTP's first hotel plan was not the log and stone resort that evolved on the shore of Lac Beauvert where Jasper Park Lodge now stands, but a grand chateau on a rise above Fiddle Creek

near Miette Hot Springs. The 1912 plans for Château Miette, drawn by Francis M. Rattenbury, featured towers, steeples and loggias to be constructed around a central garden—a design in keeping with the CPR's formal hotels at Banff and evolving at Lake Louise.

The chateau idea languished as the Dominion government mulled over the

lease agreement. As time and money slipped away, the GTP found itself struggling to complete at least the main line to the Pacific coast, let alone a chateau or any of its proposed hotels. As the rail lines approached Jasper Park, the government and foundering railway hastily made arrangements to construct a tent camp on the shores of Lac Beauvert.

The GTP turned to Fred and Jack Brewster, younger brothers of the Banff outfitting-transport siblings Bill and Jim, to select the site, and Robert Kenneth of the Edmonton Tent and Mattress Co. to finance and run "Tent City." The glorified campground opened on June 15, 1915, and 260 guests stayed in the floored cabins and ate at the dining tent that season.

But no number of tourists could curb the crisis brewing in Europe, and Tent City closed during World War I. When it reopened in 1919, Jack and Fred Brewster were the new owners. More importantly, the GTP and Canadian Northern Railway had consolidated and the government owned what the merger had created—the Canadian National Railway.

**OPENED:** JUNE 1922 (BUNGALOWS)
1923 (ORIGINAL LODGE, BURNED)
**BUILT BY:** CANADIAN NATIONAL RAILWAY
**ARCHITECTS:** JOHN SCHOFIELD & CANADIAN NATIONAL RAILWAY STAFF (ORIGINAL LODGE AND BUNGALOWS)
G.F. DRUMMOND (1953 MAIN LODGE)

Now a Crown entity, the CNR was able to circumvent much of the bureaucracy involved in securing land, and it negotiated an initial lease on 42.6 acres including the Tent City site. The railway bought out the Brewsters in 1921, upgraded the camp, added log bungalows and opened a modest "Jasper Park Lodge" in 1922.

More permanent plans were in the works. The bungalow camp would soon blossom under the direction of the CNR's flamboyant and visionary new president, American-born Sir Henry Thornton.

While Sir Henry envisioned a major destination resort at Jasper, he had no desire to replicate what the Canadian Pacific Railway had established at its hotels in Banff and Lake Louise. Instead, he decided to play upon the log camp idea already sprouting in Jasper and at some of the CPR's bungalow camp locations, including Emerald Lake Chalet and the more rustic Lake O'Hara Camp. But Jasper would not be a rustic camp, rather a perfectly planned, appointed and executed clubby resort meant to complement its surroundings.

The more sophisticated camp vernacular had a successful track record south of the border. The style had taken hold in upstate New York in the late 1800s, when men of money built clusters of cabins around lodges for private resorts

dubbed Adirondack Camps.

In addition, American railways had found that the log and stone lodges they built in that country's national parks were as popular as some of the scenery. And no wonder: the buildings seemed to grow from the ground up. Being of indigenous material, with structures in proportion to their settings and colors close to nature, the architecture became part of the outdoor experience. And it was that lure of the outdoors that drew visitors to the parks of the Canadian Rockies.

The CNR's Montreal architects, under the direction of John Schofield, began designing charming log bungalows along with pavilions and the main lodge. As Jasper Park Lodge plans were drawn, timber was harvested from the park and special cedar brought from British Columbia for what would become one of the finest examples of rustic architecture in North America.

Construction of the main building and surrounding cabins progressed

through the winter of 1922 and 1923, and Jasper Park's main lodge officially opened the following June.

And what a lodge it was! Built of peeled logs on a fieldstone foundation, the building had a low-pitched roof that extended over the verandah and was supported by stone pillars. Broad dormers protruded along the sloping roof, and bent stick braces held the tie-beams. The floor plan centered around a pivotal "rotunda" with three wings radiating from the core.

Inside, Arts & Crafts period chandeliers hung from the ceiling, and wicker furniture (like that favored by Kate Reed, who decorated the Canadian Pacific hotels) filled the lobby. Decorative interior wood carving was done by a local craftsman, Ralph James. Large stone fireplaces warmed the spaces. The dining room featured the same exposed trusses, and if diners wanted to be closer to the great outdoors, they could have their afternoon tea on the verandah off the dining room. Guests were lodged in the surrounding bungalows that featured central heat, bathrooms with hot and cold water, electric lights and telephones.

Formal lawn and gardens accentuated a park-like setting, all designed in accordance with the Parks Service's Architecture and Town Planning Division. Two-roomed cabins and double cottages

were built along flowered paths lighted by wrought-iron English lampposts. Lanterns hung at each bungalow door. The original log bungalows featured saddle-notched corners, pyramid roofs and front verandahs. Peeled log supports with bent-stick decorative braces and peeled log railings were rustic and charming.

The lodge cost $461,000 to construct; the CNR boasted that the lodge was "the largest single-storey log building in the world."

The Canadian National Railway fully appreciated the spectacular setting, and the importance of providing guests with more than first-rate accommodations. Fred and Jack Brewster were awarded outfitting concessions and ran guided trail rides out of the lodge, everything from breakfast rides to three-week trips. Not to be outdone by CPR hotels, in 1924, the CNR hired its own group of Swiss guides to lead alpinists on such expeditions as the first ascent of Mount Alberta. In 1925, a Jasper contingent of the Trail Riders of the Canadian Rockies began its tour here.

The CNR wanted to ensure that Jasper was a total resort. Sir Henry loved to ride, but he was also an avid golfer, and he wanted a premier course along the shores of Lac Beauvert. He was not alone; the Parks Branch had laid out a basic nine-hole golf course in 1922. Two years later, without funds to properly develop the course, Parks leased the site of that course and an adjacent

*The new president of the CNR, Sir Henry Thornton, preferred the idea of a rustic but luxurious retreat. The original Jasper Park Lodge became the centerpiece of one of the best examples of perfectly executed rustic architecture found in North America.*

plot of land, adding 300 acres to the lease site. Stanley Thompson & Co. was commissioned to design the course. Thompson's vision was to create an eighteen-hole course that followed the contour of the rugged landscape.

Construction was a challenge; a crew of 200 men and fifty horse teams struggled to clear the boulder- and tree-covered site. Topsoil was hauled from Edmonton and red fescue grass was planted on the fairways.

The course was officially opened on July 17, 1925. Those who play golf to-

*The park's wildlife is reflected in a variety of ways: The Moose Nook Grill Room, above; the lobby bar chandelier's varied creatures, lower left; and the real thing, an elk, lower right.*

day appreciate not only an excellent course that blends with its spectacular setting, but also the rustic imagery that still remains from the original lodge and cabins. Shelters, comfort stations, signs, tee markers and pavilions match the log and stone architecture. The totem pole at the first tee has become a landmark commemorating the Totem Pole Golf Tournament inaugurated in 1926. In 1947, Bing Crosby, who discovered Jasper Park Lodge and its golf course while filming *The Emperor Waltz*, won the tournament.

The construction of the lodge compound continued with the peeled log motif into the 1940s, and the evolution of that genre has been divided into four phases by Parks Canada historians.

While many of the original buildings were demolished, visitors strolling through the grounds see beautifully preserved examples from each phase.

From 1922 to 1926, the architects in Schofield's office designed structures of horizontal peeled-log construction with vertical mortise wall joints and saddle-notched corners. The foundations were solid fieldstone, and straight hipped roofs topped the structures. Verandahs were supported by peeled log posts with decorative bent-stick braces.

The best extant example of this period is Le Pub in the staff housing area. Built in 1924, it originally stood in front of the lodge, where it served as a boathouse and dance hall. The following year it was dismantled and moved—mi-

nus boathouse and verandah—to its current location for use as a staff recreation hall, and a swimming pool was built near the original location.

Le Pub has a one-and-one-half-story core that was the dance floor, with lower one-story levels flanking the floor for seating and refreshments. The open log-truss ceiling with stick brackets (like those in the original lodge) is a prime example of the period's style. Light flows through roof dormers, and French double doors along each side offer ventilation and exits. Some staff buildings, the power house and charming Athabasca Cottage (Honeymoon Cottage), in relative seclusion off Athabasca Drive, also date from this period.

By 1927, the CNR decided it was time to expand the lodge. The rotunda was enlarged and a ballroom and guest room wings added. Staff dormitories, a garage and twenty new bungalows were built. These bungalows varied in size and floor plans, and by the 1930 season an eight-room cabin, two ten-room cabins and a sixteen-room cabin had been constructed. While the cottages on Bungalow Row or the larger Grant House (1930) were charming, the CPR wanted to attract wealthy guests. Two "special" self-contained cottages were built: Point (1928) and Outlook (1930). In 1931,

Viewpoint, for railway executives, was constructed. All three are extant examples of what detail and elegance can do to a log cabin.

The horizontal peeled-log motif continued, but mortised vertical corner posts replaced the saddle-notched design. Concrete foundations sheathed with field stone facades and crossed-stick verandah detailing rather than

*The great hall of the original lodge epitomized everything elegantly rustic about the building.*

bent-stick railings and brackets gave the buildings a more refined air. A slight flare was added to the hipped-roof design and many of the buildings had eyebrow windows sliced along the roofs (most since removed during reroofing). The tone shifted ever so slightly from a log "fort" look to a chalet design. Swiss chalet touches like jigsawn bargeboard trim, balconies and corbelled bracing

that appealed to the worldly (and the railway hoped very wealthy) traveler were added to the "special" cabins.

Inside, the cabins have their own formal dining rooms, kitchens and servants' quarters. Tiny reading rooms tucked under the eaves, built-in bookcases and huge stone fireplaces helped to create private retreats within the resort. These cabins have served as the home-away-from-home for royalty, dignitaries and political figures including King George VI and his wife, Queen Elizabeth, and the Duke of Kent. The *faux* royalty of Hollywood also frequented the lodge either during filming or as vacationing guests. Besides Bing Crosby, celebrities associated with Jasper Park included Joan Fontaine, Robert Mitchum, Marilyn Monroe, Rita Hayworth, Dinah Shore and James Stewart.

Today, the cabins retain luxurious appointments still suited to please royalty. The hardwood floors have been carpeted and the log walls have acquired a rich caramel patina. The cabins were redecorated in 1991 and again in 1996 featuring "Grand Canadian Lodge" decor. Original chandeliers hang from the ceilings, and while most of the furniture is new, some of the wicker dates to the 1950s, and hickory and maple pieces in the

*Le Pub is one of the few remaining examples of saddle-notched log construction that was used in the early phases of Jasper Park Lodge development.*

game rooms and dining rooms are circa 1960.

Point and Outlook cabins, with their overt Swiss detailing, are located at the end of Pyramid Road; Viewpoint, the Jasper home for Sir Henry Thornton, is within easy access to the golf course. Parks historical architects consider Viewpoint one of Schofield's finest examples of the rustic vernacular and admire his sophisticated execution of log construction with its exaggerated cross-stick detailing. A billiard room was recently added, and the living and dining rooms as well as the full enclosed verandah were also refurnished.

Besides Viewpoint, Milligan Manor (1930) was built as a golfers' guest house and the golf clubhouse was constructed at about the same time. Milligan Manor was moved to its present location near the clubhouse and next to the Stanley Thompson House in 1972. The original horizontal log clubhouse, with its long verandah accessed by a series of double doors, second story dormers and boulder veneer foundation was demolished and replaced by a larger ski and golf clubhouse in 1967.

By 1930, seventy log buildings filled the land between Lac Beauvert and Lake Mildred. But as was the case across the country, the high times were ending. The Great Depression not only stunted tourism, but also lowered the fortunes of the publicly owned CNR. Along with that fall was the 1932 resignation of Sir Henry Thornton. Without his generous allocation of funds for expansion (under his direction the railway spent $2.5 million at Jasper), and his passion for Jasper Park Lodge, the resort was frozen in time.

As the country's economy recovered, Canadians and Americans were ready to hit the road and explore the Rockies. Depression relief workers had been hired to complete a gravel two-lane highway connecting Jasper to Banff and Lake Louise. In 1940, the Banff-Jasper Highway opened; later, post-war travel boomed.

Only two new buildings were constructed between the early 1930s and 1952, and comprise the third phase of early log design. A greenhouse and gardeners' house (1938) went up near Lake Mildred. Staff Dormitory L was added to the staff compound in 1941. The dormitory was the first building constructed for year-round use; its purpose was to house the Lovat Scouts, a Scottish commando regiment being trained for duty during World War II.

While the gardeners' house and dorm were of milled frame construction, the exteriors were sheathed with log slab siding and vertical posts that imitated the earlier log and mortise design. These were designed by architects in the CNR's Winnipeg engineering department.

Staff Dormitory L still houses staff. The gardeners' cottage and greenhouse, once the residence of the lodge's first gardener, William Glass, and his assistant, William Nicoll, Sr., was renovated in 1998. Two generations of the Nicolls family continued to maintain and groom the grounds of Jasper Park Lodge until 1990, when Linda Thomas-Eddie took over the job.

The renovation of Gardeners Cottage was a serious make-over. The original, simple exterior was enhanced by a new verandah and roof. Detailing, adapted from other historic cabins including Point, Outlook and Grant House, transformed it from its staff quarters status to a "special" cabin.

Inside, a great room was created for entertaining and to meet conferencing needs. There are three bedrooms and a children's bedroom along with a billiard room and sunken living room. But the cottage has not lost its roots: gardening antiques accessorize it. Historic photographs of the gardeners and grounds they created fill the walls.

The lodge, like other resort hotels, closed to the public from 1942 to 1946 during World War II. The lodge and some of buildings were winterized. Others, in keeping with a "modernization" program from the late 1940s into the 1960s, were demolished.

*A dance pavilion and boat house (now Le Pub) was drawn by CNR architects in Winnepeg in January 1924, below. It served as both along the shore, left, until it was moved to its present location in 1925, above. Le Pub pictured today, opposite page.*

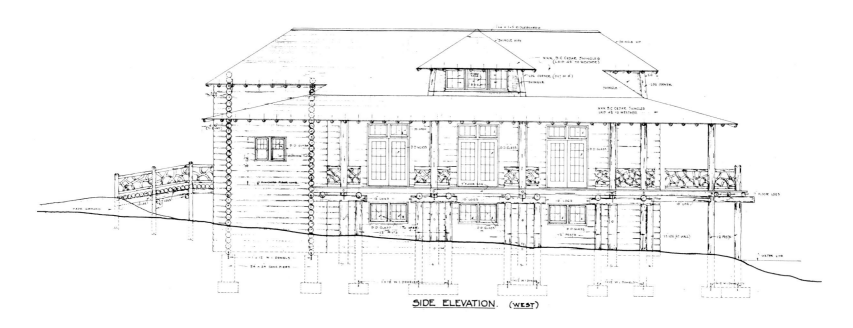

SIDE ELEVATION. (WEST)

By the late 1950s, the Banff-Jasper Highway (now Icefields Parkway) was paved, and tourist travel shifted into high gear. Expansion at Jasper Park Lodge would follow, but that development was sparked by disaster.

The loss of the most important historic structure at Jasper Park Lodge occurred on July 15, 1952. As Len Hopkins and his orchestra played in the ballroom, and music drifted into the night air, at 9:15 p.m. a fire was discovered in a checkroom of the original main lodge. Flames rippled across the varnished dance floor as guests and orchestra members raced out. Other guests playing cards in front of the massive fireplace rushed for exits. The relatively easy evacuation of the lodge was credited to its double doors accessible from each wing. Len P. Peters, Ottawa secretary to the lodge manager, was critically burned while trying to make sure all of the guests and employees had left the blazing building and save irreplaceable records. Mr. Peters later died of his burns.

The fire raged for three hours and devoured the thirty-year-old lodge and its fabulous furnishings. Firefighters and guests soon realized that there was no way to save "the largest single-storey log building in the world." As the *Edmonton Journal* reported: "As beautiful Lac Beauvert mirrored the flames, the firefighters were aided in their work by the fact that a light wind blew from the fire toward the lake, turning flames away from the threatened cabins and other buildings.

"All guests vacated the cabins, several of which were within 30 feet of the blazing log lodge. They along with the guests who escaped the lodge and the lodge employees could do little but watch the spectacle of fire.

"Viewing the fire from across the lake, many citizens were treated to an awesome spectacle of cruel beauty. A mass of orange flames and smoke billowed from the lodge, outbursts of flames now and then threatening to spread to spruce trees on either side.

"By midnight, the lodge had been destroyed. All that remained was part of the 'Tavern room' overlooking the lake, and the rock garden that a few hours earlier had bloomed near the shore. Also standing was the towering stone chimney and fireplace…"

The railway drew on all its resources, and by the next morning, the staff had set up a cafeteria-service breakfast to serve the guests, employees and firefighters. The remaining facilities stayed open for the rest of the season.

The CNR's losses were in the millions, and the impact on the area's economy could have been devastating. Rebuilding was paramount to the health of the CNR investment, and also to the well being of the entire national park.

That spark in a checkroom ended the era of rustic log construction that had become the hallmark of Jasper Park Lodge. Instead of a woodsy, rustic lodge, the Central Building, as the CNR referred to the new lodge, would reflect post-war contemporary design. Plans were submitted in August 1952 and excavation began. G.F. Drummond, chief architect for the railway, created a concrete, steel and glass structure that clearly belonged to the period, but embodied the historical references of its predecessor.

The design still pays homage to the setting by keeping a low-slung silhouette that blends with the horizon. A broad, low-pitched, gabled, cedar-shingled roof extends in exaggerated eaves

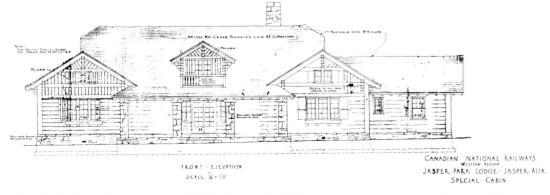

*"Special Cabin" plans drawn in 1927 by John Schofield resulted in construction of Point and Outlook that stand today.*

*The main living area of Point Cabin, with its richly patinaed peeled-log walls, Canadian lodge decor, original light fixtures, stone fireplace and detail like the bent-wood bracing, below, warrant its status as a "special cabin."*

that shade the soaring picture windows. The exterior is faced with cut fieldstone and a few sections are surfaced with log slab siding to merge it with the other log buildings. The modern lodge reflects the American architectural influence of the time and the Frank Lloyd Wrightian style rather than the rustic mountain motifs of an earlier era.

The steel framework went up in November and over 400 men worked through the winter building the lodge. The 75,000-square-foot building (forty percent larger than the original) was built in the same location. Its floor plan was in keeping with the original intent of a central lobby surrounded by wings. The sprawling building included the main lobby and business offices, entrance lobby, dining room, kitchen and assorted service areas, a ballroom, coffeeshop, anteroom and checkroom.

The $3 million Central Building opened June 9, 1953. The majestic setting was the same, but inside, contemporary architecture met historic design and dramatically brought the outdoors inside. Slate covers the entry floors, totem poles—by Canadian sculptor Arthur Price—divide the entry from the lounge and a thirty three-foot-high double-sided stone fireplace with raised hearths divides the main lobby. Atriums fill the peaked roof. On the lake side, twenty-two-by-eight-foot spans of glass separated by columns of fieldstone comprise the wall.

While the exterior remains the same, in 1989-90, the lower level of the lodge was transformed into the elegant Edith Cavell Dining Room and Beauvart Promenade to accommodate shops and entertainment arcades.

The construction of the Central Building marked the fourth phase in design at Jasper Park Lodge. In 1956, an expansion program began that altered the woodsy atmosphere of the original compound. H.C. Greensides succeeded Drummond as the CNR's architect on the Jasper project. New guest cabins and a combination ski and golf clubhouse and other buildings replaced many of the quaint log structures. Only ten of the original fifty-six log guest cabins survived the program.

Most of the modern designs used post and beam construction, and varnished exterior veneers of beveled or half-log siding combined with fieldstone facing.

Guest cabins, particularly the duplex cabins (1961-64) facing the lakefront on either side of the main lodge, replicate the design of the Central Building. The original log style was growing up, influenced by contemporary building techniques and tastes.

Fifty-three major buildings were constructed between 1952 and 1972, including many motel-style guest cabins. Also during this time, a winterization program began. The Central Building may have been stunning and modern, but it was not winterized.

In 1988, Jasper Park Lodge was acquired by a subsidiary of its old railway rival. Canadian Pacific Hotels bought the lodge compound along with the Canadian National Railway's other hotels. That year Jasper Park Lodge opened as a year-round resort.

In 1994, the Central Building was redecorated by Kerry Busby of Calgary, who has been responsible for the design work since the purchase of the lodge by CP Hotels.

*Plans for a gardener's dwelling and greenhouse were submitted by the CNR on October 26, 1938, lower right. The building would house generations of gardeners until its conversion to "special cabin" status in 1998. A great room, above, was created and accessorized with gardening tools and historic photographs.*

*The renovated exterior borrowed details from the original Outlook and Point cabins.*

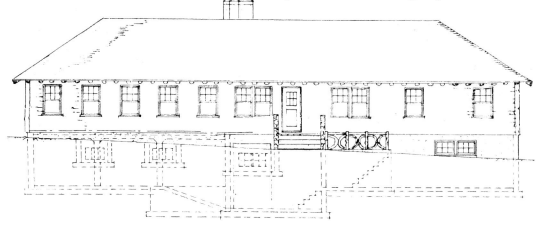

-FRONT ELEVATION-

*The Edith Cavell Dining Room, right, was created from unused space in the lower level of the lodge.*

*Totem poles divide the great hall from the reception area, below.*

*A massive stone fireplace anchors one end of the lodge's great hall redecorated in Canadian lodge motif in keeping with the original lodge decor, bottom.*

"The central lodge is classic American architecture of the day. I wanted to create the ambiance of the old lodge but not change it [the new building] architecturally," explained Busby. To do that, she took the architectural backdrop of the 1950s and married it with elements of the original grand lodge.

That backdrop included slate floors, vaulted ceilings, totem poles, Inuit artwork and massive stone fireplaces. The room was made more inviting by replacing 1960s-modern modular furnishings with styles interpreted from the original lodge furnishings.

Today, the complex has 446 guest rooms, a health spa, three dining rooms, a cafe, four lounges and convention facilities for up to a thousand visitors on 903 acres in a breathtaking setting.

Still, visitors can capture the essence of the vintage deluxe bungalow camp. Lodge Road passes under the original wooden sign. Bicycling waiters deliver room service trays. Wrought-iron lanterns glow along the paved and flower-trimmed pathways. A handful of historic log bungalows and staff buildings of exquisitely executed rustic architecture are treasures from another era.

While history buffs mourn the loss of the original log lodge and bungalows, it should be remembered that G.F. Drummond's lodge with its soaring glass and graceful lines, and the 1950s and 1960s cabins, will in time share their own historic place amidst the evolving architecture of Jasper Park Lodge.

*Bungalow Row, circa 1927, illustrates the first saddle-notched log bungalows on stone foundations with bent and burled stick detailing.*

*Athabasca Cabin, also known as "honeymoon" cabin, was set back from Bungalow Row and is one of the few remaining cabins with saddle-notched corners.*

*Outlook Cabin, with its Swiss chalet details, was built in 1929-30 as one of two "special" self-contained units.*

*Grant House was built in 1930; vertical corner posts replaced the saddle-notch design, and crossed—rather than bent—stick detailing was used along the verandah.*

*The new main lodge, constructed after the 1952 fire that destroyed the original, is a classic example of post-war architecture and set the tone for building design into the 1970s.*

*The Prince of Wales Hotel was built by the Great Northern Railway, giving the U.S. company a foothold on Canadian soil.*

There was a time in the early 1880s when plans were afoot to link the Canadian Pacific Railway via a feeder line to the Great Northern Railway in the United States. James Hill, Great Northern founder and one of the original members of the CPR syndicate's executive committee, promoted the idea. But the man Hill had hand-picked as general manager of the CPR, William Cornelius Van Horne, opposed the match made in Hill's idea of heaven. It was the beginning of Hill's defection from Canada.

Instead, James Hill and his son Louis built their own mountain nirvana with massive log lodges along the main transcontinental line of the Great Northern in Glacier National Park, Montana, adjoining Waterton Lakes National Park in Alberta 250 miles south of Banff townsite.

Waterton was established as a Canadian national park in 1895; in 1910, Glacier became a national park, thanks to the Hills' efforts. Louis Hill assumed presidency of the railway in 1907, and while his father believed that tourism would mean rail profits, it was Louis who had a burning passion for building

the great lodges and chalets. His vision was a "European" system of roads and trails through the park with a series of backcountry chalets and major hotels to serve the guests—a network finely tuned, implemented and promoted by his competitors to the north.

By 1912, Hill had secured a special Act of Congress giving the railroad the right to purchase 160 acres of the Blackfeet Indian Reservation just outside Glacier National Park. Here began a building spree that would produce Glacier Park Lodge (1913), Many Glacier Hotel (1915) and Prince of Wales Hotel (1927).

Glacier Park Lodge opened on James Hill's seventy-fifth birthday. The Glacier

hotels and chalets went up quickly, but more than a decade passed before Louis Hill realized his dream of a third major hotel in the Rocky Mountains. He had long envisioned linking the American and Canadian parks. Not only would a Canadian hotel complete his vision, but also it would root the Great Northern Railway in territory dominated by the rival CPR.

Hill picked the windswept knoll above Upper Waterton Lake in 1913, and proposed construction of a 300-room hotel. The Prince of Wales would perch high above the water on the small rise at the foot of Mount Crandell. The site offered a pedestal for the luxurious structure and a vantage point from which to view the panorama.

The idea languished for a decade. World War I broke out; Canada and then the United States joined the war effort. In 1919, the Canadian government debated damming the narrows between Upper and Middle Waterton lakes. By 1921, that idea had died, and Hill's hotel plans were reborn. But the focus and drive that were the hallmark of Glacier National Park development

**OPENED: July 25, 1927**
**BUILT BY: Great Northern Railway**
**ARCHITECT: Thomas McMahon, Great Northern Railway**
**NATIONAL HISTORIC SITE**

65

had faded in fifteen years.

Hill was challenged by new government and park regulations, and his gnawing fear that visitors might never get to this little bit of wilderness. Hill questioned whether to build the hotel at all, but finally gave the go-ahead after securing a land lease from the Canadian government in February 1926. Hill established the Canadian Rockies Hotel Company, Ltd., and plans were announced that same month that the Great Northern would build a hotel, now of 450 rooms, for $500,000.

Railway architect Thomas McMahon was commissioned to draw the plans. In May, Hill told McMahon to halt plans and withdrew funds for the hotel due to ongoing concerns about the roads. The next month everything was back on track, but McMahon was now behind schedule. In July 1926, Douglas Oland and James Scott of Oland Scott Construction of Cardston, Alberta, were contracted to build the hotel. Within days, they had a crew ready. Their deadline: July 1, 1927.

As Oland prepared the site, McMahon rushed on with the plans. Oland and Scott were accomplished builders, but the Prince of Wales would be the biggest and most complex structure of the company's history. They had just completed construction of a dance pavilion in Waterton based on plans drawn by the National Parks Branch.

The railway knew the benefits of using a local contractor. Oland threw himself into the project, working sixteen hours a day. In his handwritten memoirs, Oland recounts his early problems with finding a reliable foreman, lack of equipment and deterioration of the dirt roads. "Another drawback was the lack of good equipment, especially hoisting equipment [for] all the many timbers used, and there were a lot, [they] were hoisted by horse power. There was no good excavating equipment to get south of Calgary and the soil where I dug the basement was all large boulders in clay," he wrote. The rocks weighed from 100 to 400 pounds each.

While Oland's crew wrestled with the terrain, things were also rocky at railway headquarters in St. Paul, Minnesota. Building had started late in the season, and while the foundation work was well underway by August, exactly what the completed hotel would be was undecided. Hill called in Toltz, King & Day of St. Paul as consulting architects. As Hill and Max Toltz came up with more elaborate plans, Great Northern executives were thinking smaller. The proposed 450-room hotel plan was shrunk to sixty-five rooms. At the site, September rain had made roads impassable by truck, and Oland was hauling freight by horse and wagon. Soon snow was fall-

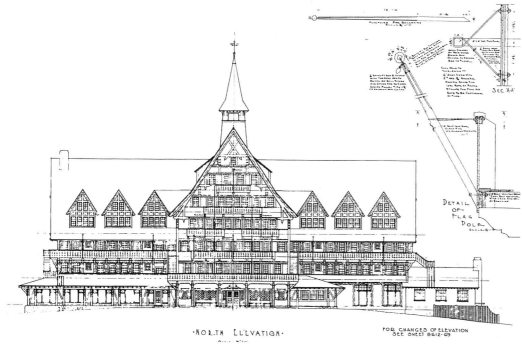

*Railway architect Thomas McMahon designed the hotel, but Louis Hill with consultants Toltz, King & Day made extensive revisions as the building went up. The final addition was a flagpole added on June 28, 1927, just in time for the opening.*

ing. Framing began and the hotel took shape through October, but by the end of the month, Oland had laid off half his building crew. Railway field accountant George Anderegg continued filing weekly reports. Timber, lumber, cement, shingles, brick and other supplies were at the site. The plans were not.

If the bean counters at the Great Northern nixed Hill's plans to expand with additional cottages and wings, Hill went in another direction. The Swiss chalet hotel plans grew—up. McMahon's concept of a four-story structure was revised to a seven-story, whimsical dollhouse. Hill was touring France and Switzerland. When he saw something he liked, his photographer would take the picture and send it back to McMahon, and the architect would again change the plans.

According to Oland's memoirs, "This meant that a lot of the structure as it now stands, had to be rebuilt four times, in early December I had walls and roof all framed, and this had to be torn down to the first floor." A fifth floor was added to the two wings, increasing guest rooms from sixty-five to ninety, which necessitated rebuilding dormers.

Wind studies had been done on the site, but defiance of the one-hundred mph gusts was almost the hotel's downfall. In December, building was going as planned and the hotel was taking shape. Built in sections, the two wings were enclosed and covered with scaffolding. On December 10, a storm blew into Waterton. Workers battened down loose material; then the wind took over. According to Oland's memoirs, the resident engineer estimated readings of an average of eighty-four mph with gusts of one hundred mph. "I would not have been too greatly surprised if the whole building had blown down, as it was, it blew eight inches off plumb," wrote Oland. Timber landed two miles away. Oland's crew winched the structure

*The view of Waterton Lakes from the great hall is the showcase of the interior.*

back within four inches of its original spot. "After that I put a lot of extra bracing in that was not called for in the plans," he continued.

Snowstorms, a second major windstorm and deterioration of the existing roads plagued the project. When trucks couldn't deliver supplies, sleighs did the job. When even sleighs or horses couldn't get through the usual route, Scott found another road.

Oland became more determined to complete the job as close to deadline as possible. Crews steadily increased, from sixty in mid-January, to ninety by the end of February, and to 125 in April. When the Great Northern recommended postponing the opening until the 1928 season, it was Douglas Oland who objected. He wrote that if they would guarantee delivery of the material and quit changing the plans, he would "give them the hotel." By June 22, 225 men were on site, and the hotel was ninety-one percent complete, according to Anderegg's weekly report. On July 25, 1927, fifteen days after Oland and Scott predicted, the Prince of Wales Hotel opened. The cost was $300,000.

What had developed on the hill overlooking Waterton Lakes was the largest wood structure in Alberta. As with the Glacier hotels, its great timbers had come by rail from the Pacific Northwest to Glacier Park Station, then moved by truck, horse or sleigh.

The hotel reinforced the Swiss chalet motif of the Great Northern's Glacier hotels, and some of the early versions of the CPR's Banff Springs Hotel and Chateau Lake Louise. But rather than using massive logs, the Prince of Wales was more refined, more European, more picturesque than any of the Great Northern's other buildings. Certainly more in keeping with the Canadian style than the log lodges in Glacier.

The interior desk and lobby show the original pictographs and hand-painted chandeliers reflecting the native peoples of the area, left. The chandeliers were moved to Lake McDonald Lodge, and the great hall was redecorated over time, below.

The hotel's core is the seven-story great hall lobby section flanked by two five-story wings and a single-story kitchen annex. The steeply-pitched gabled roofs are dotted with peaked dormers, and tiers of bracketed balconies cascade down the upper levels. A cupola and weather vane top the "cuckoo clock" design. Balcony balustrades are jigsawn, and unlike the other Great Northern lodges, the huge timbers are peeled and hand-planed. Originally, the cedar roof was meant to weather. It was painted in the 1950s and replaced in 1994 with a dark green, fireproof composite tile roof. The contrasting exterior paint emphasizes the structural detail. An extended second-floor balcony over the entrance offers shelter for arriving guests.

The Prince of Wales Hotel exterior seems like a fairy-tale creation, but it is also a shelter from which to view the park. Eighteen-foot-high windows along the lake-view side of the great hall frame a scene that none of Hill's artists hired to promote the hotels could possibly capture. Every window, from the attic to the cocktail lounge, contains the spectacular surroundings.

The great hall is far more refined than those of its Glacier counterparts. The architecture of the Canadian parks was rustic-Tudor, while to the south the rusticity reflected the "Wild West." The interior of Prince of Wales features the Tudor theme. The timber-framed lobby rises to a seventh-floor ceiling that serves as a crawl space. Access to the chandelier is from a small trap door in the ceiling, and for many years, the smallest bellman was lowered through it to change bulbs and clean the fixture. The columns and trusses that fill the lobby are all hand-hewn, and the wood is fitted and pegged together. Iron butterfly hinges and plates reinforce the joists. A second-floor balcony fills two sides of the lobby with jigsawn balustrades. Each floor has a balustrade balcony or windows from the stairs that lead to the upper-floor attic rooms.

Oland bid to build ninety bedroom suites and other furniture when his crew was bogged down by the weather or changes in plans. Hill selected most of the furnishings in Winnipeg instead, but the decorating details reflected the real heritage of the area. Pictographs painted by Blood Indian elders filled the lobby. Hand-painted lanterns with the same designs hung from the rafters.

The one-story dining room was always elegantly appointed. Windows flank the north wall, but the scene does not dominate the room. Wainscoting covers the lower walls with plasterboard above.

The guest rooms are charming, many with balconies and lovely views. The fifth- and sixth-floor rooms feature tiny alcoves, and access up narrow stairways gives the feeling of climbing into a very fancy tree house.

While all the hotels suffered from financial difficulties prompted by the Depression, Prince of Wales' location along with poor roads plagued it. In 1930, Bill Brewster—who had left Banff's Brewster Transport and was operating Glacier Park Transportation Company—along with the CPR and the Great Northern Railway began a rail and motor tour known as Rawhide Trail Tours. The plan was for tourists to travel by rail from Chicago to the Rockies and return using both CPR and Great Northern trains and staying at the railways' hotels. Passengers would travel from Chicago to Glacier National Park on the Great Northern and then transfer to the Prince of Wales Hotel in Glacier Park Transportation Company coaches. From Waterton, they would take Brewster Transport's eighteen-seat coaches to Banff where they would eventually head home via the CPR.

As the railways were putting together the plans, an unusual alliance between the United States and Canada was growing. The International Rotary Clubs proposed to join Waterton and Glacier as an International Peace Park. In 1932, the peace park was dedicated. As symbolic as the park joining was, it could not stave off the effects of the De-

pression. In 1933, the railway did not open the hotel for the season. It would remain closed for two years, during which it suffered the ravages of neglect and weather. The closure was a blow to the town of Waterton and the Rotarians, but it pushed the completion of Chief Mountain Highway linking Glacier National Park to Waterton Lakes Park. When the hotel reopened, visitors from the United States could more easily drive to the Canadian hotel.

The Prince of Wales Hotel was labeled early on as a haven for Americans made liquorless by Prohibition. A beer hall off the lobby (replaced by a gift shop in the 1950s) became Waterton's first bar. The original first floor of the Prince of Wales Hotel went through a number of changes, most made in the 1950s while the railway was renovating its hotels with hopes of selling. There was really no one to object. Louis Hill died in 1948, and with him the passion and understanding of his Glacier/Waterton developments.

The Windsor Lounge was eventually added on the lobby's east side, resulting in an unfortunate reworking of the once stately fireplace. The elegant double-sided stairway was partially enclosed, but the tiny elevator is the oldest running elevator in Alberta. The Indian pictographs were removed and some of the lanterns were moved to Lake Mc-Donald Lodge in Glacier National Park and replaced by three-tiered aluminum chandeliers. Repairs to the timber columns have been made with care; all are hand-planed and honeycombed to replicate the original. The electrical system, fire escapes, sprinkler system, and kitchen were updated.

Prince of Wales Hotel was placed under the management of Donald Knutson of Minneapolis in 1957. In 1960, Donald Hummel acquired the Prince of Wales along with the Glacier Park hotels. Today, Glacier Park, Inc., a subsidiary of Viad Corp, owns and operates the hotel on land leased from Parks Canada.

Between 1993 and 1995, Glacier Park, Inc., did the aforementioned re-roofing, replaced windows with thermal pane, and updated bathrooms. In 1996, GPI revived earlier plans to expand the hotel. Any additions must be in keeping with the historic integrity of the Prince of Wales Hotel and be part of the total Waterton Lakes Framework for Managing Development Plan, according to Parks Canada.

The Prince of Wales Hotel, whose namesake never saw the building, is a fitting monument to both Louis Hill and his father. The immeasurable impact James Hill had on American and Canadian settlement, development and prosperity through his railway enterprises cannot be measured. Perhaps his son built this odd duck of a hotel as a memorial to his Canadian-born father who dreamed, schemed, bullied and brainstormed his way through two countries.

*The tiny red elevator is the oldest operating elevator in Alberta. The hotel's designation as a National Historic Site is displayed next to it, right.*

*The dining room, below, offers lovely views of Waterton Lake.*

The hotel takes on a magical light in the night.

The Prince of Wales Hotel is reflected in Linnet Lake, right.

## Lodge Retreats

OFF THE BEATEN PATH—BUT NOT TOO FAR—
THESE LODGES AND CABINS OFFER THE AMBIANCE OF
A BACKCOUNTRY EXPERIENCE WITHOUT THE HIKE.
EMERALD LAKE AND LAKE O'HARA LODGES WERE
DEVELOPED INTO THE CANADIAN PACIFIC RAILWAY'S
DELUXE BUNGALOW CAMPS; NUM-TI-JAH IS ONE
OF THE FEW HISTORIC LODGES OUTSIDE OF
TOWNSITES NOT BUILT BY A RAILWAY.

*Num-Ti-Jah Lodge and Bow Lake, Banff National Park.*

The summer of 1882 was a season of discovery. Tom Wilson, a horse-packer working on a Canadian Pacific Railway survey, is credited as the first non-native to gaze upon both Lake Louise and Emerald Lake. Today, that summer seems like a season made in heaven. But in the halcyon years between 1881, when a rail route through the mountains was established, to well past the turn of the 20th century, one delicious discovery after another was melting on the palates of those with a taste for adventure. The Canadian mountains offered a smorgasbord of tantalizing challenges.

By the early 1900s, a frenzy of tourism had built up in the mountains surrounding the CPR's line. Banff Springs Hotel, Lake Louise Chalet, Glacier House and Mount Stephen House had all been expanded to meet tourist demands. Travel writers were penning glowing descriptions, alpinists achieving first ascents and, along the way, amateur scientists were making important discoveries. In 1899, the railway hired Swiss guides for climbers, and peaks, mountain passes and plants were being identified and named. Members of the prestigious Alpine Club of London and the Appalachian Mountain Club of Boston returned each season to revel in the glory of it all.

Local outfitters were in hog heaven, and the CPR was promoting the adventure with the gusto of pigs at the trough. And why not?—even with the tough economic climate of the mid-1890s,

these were exciting times. The railway found itself catering to tourists bent on forging beyond the old "resort" idea. They were adventuresome men and women of means, and if the railway wanted them as repeat customers, it would have to build additional facilities—off the beaten track.

In 1902, the CPR requested title to about four acres on the shores of Emerald Lake in newly formed Yoho Park Reserve and requested that the plot be surveyed. It was a setting of marvelous confluence. A jewel of a lake dropped at the foot of limestone peaks with a peninsula on which to build a Swiss-styled chalet. The railway allocated $10,000 to build its first "backcountry" chalet, whose design would reflect the railway's pitch that the Rockies were the Swiss Alps of Canada, enticing travelers to use CPR ships and trains. The construction site was seven miles from Field, where trains stopped at a small station on the CPR's main line, and guests hiked or rode horseback into the chalet.

This was the company's initial development in Yoho Park Reserve, and it took three years of negotiations before the CPR was issued a forty-two-year lease to 13.44 acres on which Emerald Lake Chalet had already been built. Annual rent was $100. When it seemed the lease agreement would finally be resolved, the Department of the Interior decided that all leases would be forfeited in Yoho Park if liquor was sold on the premises. CPR's Charles Drinkwa-

*Guests await their carriage on the porch of the Emerald Lake Chalet before its expansion.*

ter, who had been negotiating the lease, was dumbfounded. "As you no doubt fully understand, the purposes for which this chalet was built was to induce tourist travel to the park, and to prohibit the sale of wines and liquors would, I fear, greatly militate against the success of our efforts," he wrote.

A month later, an agreement was reached, and spirits could be sold at the chalet. Any animosity that developed over the negotiating period was discreetly veiled in the 1905 report of Su-

perintendent Howard Douglas: "The Canadian Pacific Railway Company, with commendable foresight and enterprise, lost no time in erecting on the borders of the lake a handsome and most comfortable chalet, which even now has become inadequate for the accommodation of many visitors who make Emerald Lake the objective point of their progress through the park, and so popular has this favored spot already become that it is intended to at least double the capacity of the chalet (now only a year old) the coming winter."

The approved drawings submitted by the CPR chief assistant engineer's office in Montreal, in 1902, show a two-and-one-half story building with eleven

second-floor bedrooms with shared baths and a main floor with a dining room, small entry/lounge, extra bedrooms, offices, kitchen and food storage areas. A proposed extension of the dining room was already sketched in place. The design had many of the proportions and exterior features of a European chalet, combined with the rustic log construction popular in the Adirondacks summer camps of upstate New York built in the 1870s.

The chalet had a gabled roof with exaggerated overhangs supported by corbels, and peeled log columns held the balcony. Constructed from hand-hewn squared timbers instead of logs, the style was ideal for the wooded, remote and dazzling setting. While it had the feeling of a Swiss chalet it did not feature overt detailing such as jigsawn decorative trim and balustrades.

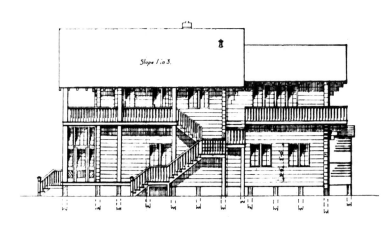

Side Elevation.

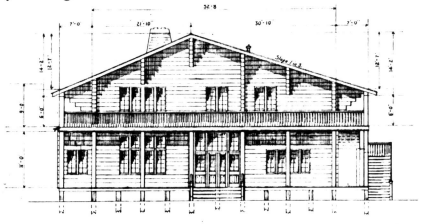

Front Elevation.

*Plans were drawn in 1902 by architects in the CPR's Montreal engineering department for the railway's first "backcountry" chalet.*

The dining room featured hardwood floors, wainscoting, a beamed ceiling and banks of multi-paned windows. By day, sunlight streamed in through the windows and, as dusk approached, kerosene chandeliers were lighted to bathe the room in a soft glow.

By 1906, 805 registered guests had enjoyed a stay at the chalet. The railway added cabins along the lakefront and surrounding forest. Some of the original cabins were built on the lake's edge before the 1909 park regulation requiring buildings to be 100 feet from any body of water. The charming chalet and cabins grew in popularity, and the Interior Department reported 1,192 guests during the 1912 season (sixty-six percent from the USA, twenty-five percent from Canada, six percent from England and three percent other). By 1913, that number had nearly doubled with 2,260 registered guests. As with the other CPR hotels, guest registration dropped with the onset of World War I, but recovered by 1915.

Emerald Lake Chalet was initially designed as a hotel, but the addition of individual log cabins gave it a new appeal. It was an appeal that would be played out between 1919 and 1926 in a series of bungalow camps the CPR built to link bridle trails, hiking routes and roadways through the Rockies. Each camp featured a community building for eating and socializing that was surrounded by simple log cabins.

Growing automobile road access to once-remote reaches of the parks

*In 1925, CPR's Basil Gardom submitted plans for the expansion of the chalet. The completed addition emphasized the Swiss theme the railway was promoting in the parks.*

brought the "bungalow camp" to the roadside. A road opened to Emerald Lake Chalet in 1920, and guests could drive in by automobile.

What evolved at Emerald Lake was not a traditional bungalow camp, rather "The Camp de Luxe" as the marketing department dubbed it. Additions to the site were made in 1922 and 1925, including more bungalows and a clubhouse featuring hardwood floors "kept in splendid condition for dancing" and furnished with writing desks, card tables, a piano, wicker furniture and record player to create an auxiliary oasis for recreation and socializing.

The log bungalows each had a moderately-pitched gable roof with a broad overhang covering a spacious verandah. Inside, there were hardwood floors,

electric light, running water and "a funny little drum stove" as a 1924 brochure described it.

No doubt spurred by the popularity of the Emerald Lake Chalet "camp de luxe" and Jasper Park Lodge, built by the Canadian National Railway in 1922-23 in the northern reaches of the Rocky Mountains, the CPR decided to expand two of its camp facilities.

In the railway's Montreal Engineering Department, architects were working on plans to enlarge Emerald Lake Chalet and to build a new central lodge for Lake O'Hara, a log bungalow camp also in Yoho National Park. When completed, these two, while still referred to as "bungalow camps," became the more luxurious backcountry retreats of the railway's hotel empire.

*Cilantro on the Lake and the new cottages are part of the modernization of Emerald Lake Lodge.*

In 1925, Basil Gardom submitted plans that would nearly double the size of the chalet. Gardom shipped in sawn ten-by-ten squared cedar lumber for the Emerald Lake addition. The expanded chalet housed an enlarged dining room, kitchen, offices, staff dining hall, and ice and vegetable store rooms plus a new wing of guest rooms. Along with the expansion, running water and improvements to the bedrooms to the old portion were completed. The Swiss styling of the original structure was followed in the expansion. Simple railings and vertical wood balustrades enclosed the balconies, and flowering baskets were hung around the perimeter. A large fieldstone fireplace was added to the dining space.

Inside, the dining room was finished with wainscoting and lath and plaster walls. Wooden Arts & Craft style chairs surrounded linen covered tables, and tulip-shaped light fixtures hung from the beamed ceiling. The bedroom walls were also finished with lath and plaster, and simple flowered curtains dressed the windows.

During this time the CPR was not the only company staking business claims around the lake. Two livery stables were operating, one by Brewster Transport Company and the other by Wesley Patrick Sheek, a local guide.

Still, Emerald Lake was a tranquil location. Now easier to access than the backcountry lodges only available to those willing to hike, ski or ride horseback into the wild, yet away from the main tourist attractions of Banff and Lake Louise. It seemed idyllic.

But the Great Depression would change the fortunes of many, and when travelers picked up the shards of broken dreams, their tastes had changed. Shaken by the Depression, thrifty travelers of the 1930s began pitching their own tents in the growing number of campgrounds rather than pulling into bungalow camps. CPR divested itself of its tea houses and small bungalow camps, but kept its two grand hotels and Emerald Lake Chalet. The chalet was closed during World War II, but after the war business prospects seemed good enough for the CPR to enter into another lease—the rent would remain at $100 a year. In 1951, an application for the addition of bathrooms to the two-roomed cabins along with construction of a diesel house and work shop was submitted; approval came two years later.

The CPR continued to operate Emerald Lake Chalet until 1959, when the lease was transferred to Brewster Transport Company Ltd. In 1971, the property again changed hands to John A. Smith Management, Ltd., and two years later to Beaver Industries, Ltd.

Finally, in 1978, Pat O'Connor and Michael Laub (now Canadian Rocky Mountain Resorts) entered into another lease. Emerald Lake Chalet and Cabins was under a cease operation notice from Parks Canada, and O'Connor was about to embark on a total redevelopment of the property that would go on for eight years. It took three years to work out a permit, and as the economy took a downturn the project was discontinued,

*As was the case in the original chalet, the renovated Emerald Lounge is brimming with cozy and comfortable chairs.*

*A new boathouse and dock, right, are available to guests to loll away summer afternoons on Emerald Lake.*

*Flower baskets brighten the entrance and suggest the Swiss chalet motif still prevalent in the lodge's exterior, below.*

then merely scaled back. A second approval process was undertaken, and in 1984, demolition of the twenty-one original cabins and construction began. The facility reopened in June 1986, as Emerald Lake Lodge and Conference Center.

The new cabins on the west end of the property were placed on the footprints of the original buildings. Log construction was not feasible, so twenty-four two-story clapboard cabins creating eighty-five units were built. They feature balconies and river rock fireplaces, and some of the lower level rooms have separate sitting rooms. A clubhouse and outdoor hot tub, exercise room and sauna are modern-day additions. Cilantro on the Lake, a summer restaurant and meeting facility, was also added to the property. The tiny boathouse, now closed, is the only other remaining original structure besides the main building.

The main lodge exterior looks very much the same as it did in the heyday of the late 1920s. A portion of the first level verandah was enclosed with glass to extend the dining area. The roof was raised slightly to accommodate insulation. Rotted wood railing and supports were replaced retaining the original style. The addition of Kicking Horse Lounge off the kitchen on the main floor is the only new construction. But inside, the building was gutted.

Old plaster and lathing were removed to uncover the original rough-hewn ce-

*The second floor was once guest rooms. During renovation, the upper level ceilings were removed exposing the timbers and structural beams of what is now the Billiard Room.*

dar timber. The lobby features hardwood floors, the original river rock fireplace, three walls of uncovered rough-hewn cedar paneling and a new oak stairway. The Burgess Dining Room has more of the cedar-paneled walls with simple period light fixtures. Upholstered chairs and elegant linen and service bring back the days of the CPR. Additional dining on the glass-enclosed verandah is delightful, with fabulous views of Emerald Lake and mounts Burgess and Wapta.

A 1924 CPR brochure written by Madge Macbeth describing the chalet could have been the inspiration for the renovation of the Emerald Lounge: "But it was not the picturesqueness of the place, or the harmonious blending with the surroundings, that impressed me most; it was not the two spacious verandahs, nor the color scheme carried right into the dining room, where smart maids wore green ribbons on their caps; it was not the excellence of the table, where fresh fruit and vegetables were served in colossal quantities, nor the courtesy of the entire staff. It was the remarkable fact that there was always a sufficiency of comfortable chairs!"

The new Emerald Lounge is brimming with comfortable chairs! Bent willow chairs, ladder-back chairs, overstuffed chairs, wicker rocking chairs and traditional camel-back sofas. There are seating areas galore—by the stone fireplace, corner windows and lake-view vantage spots.

The butterscotch-colored Kicking Horse Lounge off Emerald Lounge is a new addition, but the back bar is an antique shipped from the Yukon.

The upper floor of the chalet was originally guest rooms with men's and women's lavatories. The old ceiling was removed to expose the timbers and four foot main structural beams, and walls were cleared leaving structure timbers and some of the cedar walls. Notches cut along the upper wall line are still visible where cross beams once held the lower ceiling.

Today, the Yoho Lounge is flanked by two meeting rooms (The President and The Vice President). A stone fireplace was added that divides the Lounge from

the Billiard Room. A bison head mounted on the stone chimney-piece fills nearly half of the Billiard Room wall. The antique pool table, piano and chess tables are reminiscent of the old Clubhouse ambiance. Office space is housed in the back of the building.

The second story verandah, where guests once enjoyed afternoon tea, is still open. The view remains as breathtaking as in 1903.

What has changed is access to the lodge. Parking is below the facility. During the permit negotiations dealing with the head lease site, Canadian Rocky Mountain Resorts wanted to move the industrial components away from the chalet and cabins. The compa-

*The simple Arts & Crafts period dining room, above, was transformed into the elegant Burgess Dining Room, and the verandah enclosed for additional space.*
*The remarkable view of The President and The Vice President peaks from the original second-floor balcony, right, remains the same.*

ny took over what had once been a gravel quarry in exchange for tree-filled land on the original site. That gave them the ability to move all of the services, staff housing and guest parking away from the main lodge. A van transports guests to the lodge and cabins sited in an area free of the congestion from cars.

Emerald Lake Lodge is open year round, and guests seem startled to find themselves on a peninsula of a snow-covered or shamrock-colored lake in a Swiss chalet in British Columbia. Fires roar, warming the charming rooms, and guests dine on exquisite contemporary fare. The wait staff is outfitted circa 1920, and even after renovation there is something decidedly old about the place. It could be the hand-hewn cedar timbers of the

original lodge or the smooth stone of the fireplaces. Perhaps it's the aged chinking poking between the boards or the moss that grows from the roof shingles like green whiskers.

But once settled in a comfy chair, guests gaze out at the scenery and know that it is the setting. The shale fossil beds of Mount Burgess, the peaks of The President and The Vice President, the lake—the ever tantalizing lake. The scene recalls those halcyon days of discovery. Those days when Victorian ladies and gentlemen enjoyed what seemed like such ungenteel behavior as they hoisted themselves over rocks, snow fields and glaciers. And when they returned from another great adventure, they took refuge in places like Emerald Lake Chalet.

*Ordaray Mountain looms above Lake O'Hara Lodge and Cabins mirrored in the calm lake waters.*

If you must have the glories of Rocky Mountain scenery plus such trappings of modern luxury as magnificent hotels, elaborate meals, dance halls, golf courses, automobiles and swarms of visitors, go to Banff or Louise. O'Hara's appeal is rather to those who prefer to take their scenery straight."

*Bungalow Camps in the Canadian Pacific Rockies,* 1927

Over seventy years later, much of Lake O'Hara Lodge's appeal is the same. The dirt road to the lake is still off limits to cars. Summer visitors can walk, but most overnight guests board a shuttle bus that transports them from a parking lot off the Trans Canada Highway to another time.

There is a flash of blue green between the fir and spruce trees. The yellow school bus halts, and passengers are deposited at the northwest bay of Lake O'Hara. Nature's peep show does not disappoint, for up the path the lake water fills a bowl of limestone against mountains that cut a Rorschach silhouette against the sky. Wiwaxy Peaks and Yukness Mountain are near bookends. Mount Huber stands between them with other peaks punctuating the Continental

Divide. Seven Sisters Falls releases the flow of Lake Oesa from a slit in the jumbled moraine and the water rumbles to the shoreline.

It was from a higher vantage point that J.J. McArthur, a Dominion land surveyor working on a preliminary topographical survey of the region for the

Canadian Pacific Railway, spotted Lake O'Hara in 1887. Lake McArthur became his own namesake, but the better known Lake O'Hara bears the moniker of an Irish tourist, Lieutenant-Colonel Robert O'Hara, who hiked the region in the 1890s.

At the time, the CPR had its hands full fighting political battles, operating a

railway and constructing hotels and train stations across Canada, but a setting this magnificent did not go unnoticed. In 1909, the Alpine Club of Canada held its annual summer camp at Lake O'Hara, and nearly 200 alpinists pitched tents in the meadow beneath Mount Schäffer.

Soon after Yoho was designated a national park in 1911, Wiwaxy Lodge, one of the oldest known backcountry shelters in the national parks, was constructed at the Alpine Meadow near the lake. The peeled log cabin met the basic needs of hikers, many crossing the Continental Divide between Lake Louise and Lake O'Hara.

By 1919, the area had received the attention of more hikers and trail riders, and the CPR built a larger lodge nearby, later renamed the Elizabeth Parker Hut. Construction of the lodge and surrounding tent cabins at the Alpine Meadow marked one of the railway's first forays into development of "bungalow camps." The tent cabins were soon replaced by simple log cabins, and the backcountry camp became a stop on the railway's Bungalow Camp Tour.

Bungalow camps fit the travel tastes of the era, and the railway aggressively met the public's changing vacation needs and the parks' road expansion project. By the mid-1920s, the CPR was operating the much-expanded Chateau Lake Louise, rebuilding and enlarging Banff Springs Hotel, had added cabins and a clubhouse to Emerald Lake Chalet, was constructing log bungalow camps along new roadways, and building tea houses and rest houses on backcountry trails—all part of its expanding camp tour network.

Broadening the "camp de luxe" idea

was also in the works, and the railway's Montreal Engineering Department drew up plans for a new main lodge at Lake O'Hara and an addition at Emerald Lake Chalet.

The CPR had acquired a lease in the Alpine Meadow above Lake O'Hara, but they wanted the new lodge to be located near the shoreline where the lake's pristine waters mirrored the breathtaking mountain panorama. After some confusion and correspondence, the company secured a lease of five acres on the north shore, and the meadow lease was eventually transferred to the Alpine Club of Canada.

Blueprints for the new lodge were

submitted, but construction was delayed for a year. Plans were resubmitted in September and again in December 1925, by Basil Gardom to the park superintendent. Drafts for the $10,000 lodge were revised and finally approved by J.B. Harkin, Commissioner of Dominion Parks in Ottawa. At this time, under his leadership, Dominion Parks was establishing design guidelines for public and private buildings in the parks, and officials were becoming more active in their role as architectural critics.

The CPR may have been torn on the style of architecture to use for the new lodge. On one hand, the Canadian Na-

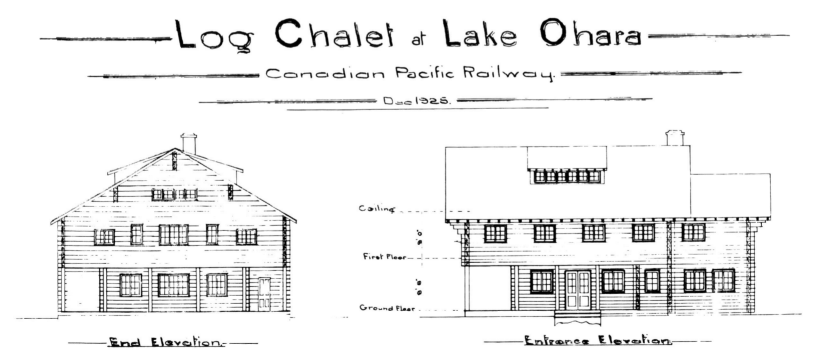

*Plans for a chalet at Lake O'Hara were submitted in September and again in December 1925. The Commissioner of Dominion Parks approved the revised drawings with fewer bedrooms and no card room.*

*A window frames perfection and was given to the lodge by Dr. George "Tommy" Link. It was dedicated in 1971 as a place "to look, to think and to wonder."*

*Lake O'Hara Camp, below, was built in a meadow away from the lake. The cabins were skidded to the shoreline to accompany the new lodge; today, Elizabeth Park Hut and Wiwaxy Lodge remain in the meadow.*

tional Railway was successfully creating a sophisticated bungalow camp using the rustic log vernacular in Jasper National Park, yet the CPR had been promoting the Canadian Rockies as the Canadian Alps, and a Swiss chalet motif reinforced that campaign.

Architects settled on a substantial but basic Swiss chalet design for both the new Lake O'Hara Lodge and the Emerald Lake Chalet addition. Instead of jig-sawn detailing, the European flavor was achieved through the use of squared timber construction, and milled brackets, rails and rafters. Five- and seven-step corbelled brackets supporting expansive roof overhangs, exposed timbers and a balcony off the second floor under the gabled roof alluded to European design. The milled log work was more formal than peeled logs, while still blending with the wooded mountain setting.

Crews had prepared the trail to accommodate transport of building supplies, and work began in the fall of 1925. As with Emerald Lake Chalet, squared Douglas-fir was shipped by rail from Vancouver then hauled by horse-drawn wagon or sleigh from the Hector station to the lake site. Banff outfitter George Harrison was hired as foreman, and a crew of about fifteen men worked on the lodge through the winter. Harrison and his wife Nellie lived in a cabin at the meadow during the seven months. And while hauling supplies and materials to the site was difficult, the setting made it worthwhile. In a 1970 taped audio interview, Nellie Harrison recalled:

"…Oh, it was beautiful! The sun shone most of the time, and snow! Well you couldn't move without going on skis. We skied all winter...just around the valley there, and we went up to Lake McArthur. We had Christmas dinner right in the middle of the lake. Oh, it was a beautiful day, and everything was just like fairyland!...And the trees were all hanging with the hoar frost, and the sun was out so bright; it was just beautiful! I don't think I have ever seen a prettier picture."

The resulting lodge is a two-and-one-half-story rectangular building topped with a bellcast split-cedar shingled roof.

The narrower kitchen wing is off the back of the lodge with a slightly lower roof line. Single shed dormers (originally designed as double dormers) project from each side of the main roof and flood the open great hall corridor with light. Patchwork panes of pink, green, yellow and clear glass fill the dormer windows.

Originally, verandahs surrounded three sides of the building at ground level. Unlike at Emerald Lake Chalet, second floor bedrooms rather than balconies were built over the verandah and were supported by squared timber columns.

Today, diners fill two of the enclosed verandahs where they enjoy notable gourmet fare. From this premier space they watch the high summer sun slowly make its way over the Continental Divide. Or in the winter, guests catch the early dusk as darkness cloaks the snow-covered landscape. The forest has matured since the lodge's construction and only slivers of the glacial lake can be seen from the first floor. The enclosure of the verandahs is noticeable only to those who have seen historic photographs; large paned windows were inserted between the original columns, and horizontal boards reflect the style and tone of the original structure.

In the mid 1980s, a new entrance was designed. Guests now enter the lodge from the south corner onto a small two-level porch and into a vestibule. Harris Bertzloff of Canmore, Alberta designed the addition with the owners; the plan was then approved by the park superintendent. Using one-by-ten Douglas-fir, stained to match the original finish, the addition adheres to the building's architectural integrity. With it, a cherry wood reception desk and pillars were added to the lobby.

*The open lounge has always been a gathering place for guests.*

To visitors, the simplicity of the original design seems untouched, and the lodge's ambiance is the same as in 1926. The central great hall is bathed in gentle light from the dormers and first floor windows. Interior walls throughout are still covered in white painted plywood with dark brown lathing resembling plaster and lath, creating a lovely contrast to the natural wood ceiling. Oil lamps were used until a generator was installed in 1931.

The central hall is a gathering place for guests to dine, relax or read, but mostly to plan the day's activities. After a vigorous or leisurely hike comes afternoon tea, then dinner is announced by a gong's ringing. Like invited guests at a dinner party, everyone slowly migrates to the living room after dessert and gathers around the huge stone fireplace whose mantle holds a collection of crystals, fossils and the heel of a lady's 1920s era hob-nailed boot. Conversations of hiking, geology and history prevail.

An open balcony encircles the second floor from which eight simple guest rooms, men's and women's bathrooms and storage are accessed. But it is far more than a hallway. A gallery of historic photos and small library add to the charm. At the balcony's far end, a sofa, chairs and a desk are arranged behind a large picture window. That window says much about Lake O'Hara Lodge. It was presented to the lodge by Dr. George "Tommy" Link in memory of his first wife, Adeline DeSale, and Margaret Ervin Schevill, his second wife. Both women played important roles in executing his plan to make the south area of Lake O'Hara accessible to hikers. Over fifty years, Link—along with others, most notably Lawrence Grassi and Carson Simpson—built a network of trails that fan from the lodge. The window was dedicated in 1971 by Dr. Charles Fielding as a place "to look, to think, and to wonder."

the new site, that they were to be placed on the new area leased, so that the Company have no cause for complaint if they should be asked to remove them from their present position…"

Once in place, the cabins remained.

The eleven one-room cabins are built of peeled spruce logs. Originally placed on stone foundations, they now rest on steel I-beams with rock facade foundations. Each cabin offers a personal rustic retreat, and each was originally intended to reinforce the sense of adventure in the woods and mountains. That adventure included finding one's way to an outhouse. As noted in a 1928 *Bungalow Camps in the Canadian Pacific Rockies* brochure: "You can either sleep in the Chalet or in one of the little log-cabins that are strewn on the lake shore—together they will accommodate about 38 guests. Some people prefer the Chalet because there is a real bathroom there with hot and cold water, while others like the idea of going to sleep in a little house of their own and watching the moonlight shining across the placid lake." Real bathrooms—with hot and cold water—were eventually added to the cabins.

The pot-bellied wood-burning stoves of the past were replaced by propane heat. Small paned windows, open ceilings, log walls and wooden floors reflect the same rustic design as the exterior. Each cabin has saddle-notched corners and a pitched roof that extends over individual front porches outfitted

While the main lodge architecturally dominates the site, the log cabins have their own historic charm. The original cabins from the Alpine Meadow camp were skidded across the snow and placed along the shoreline during the winter of 1926-27. The two larger log huts were left in the meadow where they remain today. Numbers vary on exactly how many cabins were moved and when, but one thing is apparent, CPR wanted the cabins on the shore.

Structures in the national park were not allowed within 100 feet of the water. In 1929, Yoho and Glacier Park Superintendent E.W. Russell wrote memos of outrage to his superior in Ottawa, J.B. Harkin, trying to explain the matter: "The buildings now on the shores of Lake O'Hara are of course not on the C.P.R. leased ground, and were placed without my knowledge or approval. The understanding was, when the buildings were removed from the old camp site to

*Hikers on a trail above Lake O'Hara Lodge, right.*

*The lodge, now surrounded by mature trees, has a new entry and enclosed verandahs, but the charm and ambiance is from another time, below.*

with wicker or rocking chairs. There is no interior ornamentation unless you count the shipping instructions: *Basil Gardom, Hector Station* scrawled on one ceiling board.

Numerous storage and staff buildings have come and gone. In addition to the eleven lakeshore cabins, there are four contemporary units in two duplex cabins located on a shelf of land overlooking the lake. The access road was used only as a walking or horse trail until the 1950s, when a shuttle bus was allowed to ferry visitors to the lodge and campground. Today, an allotted number of visitors can be transported into the fragile wilderness. During the winter, guests cross-country ski or snowshoe to the lodge.

The CPR continued to operate Lake O'Hara and its other backcountry lodges and tea houses until they became a financial burden. The lodge was closed from 1942 to 1945 during World War II, and Swiss guide Edward Feuz and his son were caretakers. In 1944, the CPR's law department sent a memorandum in preparation for post-war lease agreements showing the capital investment in Lake O'Hara and Twin Falls Tea House. As of December 31, 1943, the company noted a total deficit of $21,194.57 for Lake O'Hara with a capital investment of $49,119.

In September 1953, R.A. Mackie, General Manager of [CPR] Hotels, wrote National Parks Director J.A. Hutchison that the company had no in-tention of disposing of its operation at Lake O'Hara "which is well patronized by people coming to the Canadian Rockies by train." But Mackie was negotiating to sell the properties to Claude Brewster, and by the spring of 1954, the Canadian Pacific Railway Company indeed sold Lake O'Hara Lodge along with Wapta Lodge, Yoho Valley Lodge and Twin Falls Tea House to Brewster and Ford Mountain Lodges Limited, formed by Claude Brewster and Austin Ford.

The Brewster family's enterprises dominated the region, and Sylvia (Sid) Brewster had run the original camp then Lake O'Hara Lodge from the 1920-21

*The original verandahs were enclosed over time to accommodate dining space, but little has changed except the diners' attire.*

season until her death in 1953. In 1930, she married Sidney Graves, and he helped with the lodge until his death in 1945. The Brewsters and Fords co-owned the lodge until 1957, when Austin and Phyllis Ford became the sole proprietors. The Ford family operated the lodge until 1975 when it was sold to Ekstrand Holdings, Ltd. and operated by Michael and Marsha Laub with Tim and Leslee Wake. Presently the lodge is run by Alison and Bruce Millar with the assistance of Carman Haase and Charly Gasser.

It is the summer of 1998, and guests have enjoyed dinner of toasted barley and mushroom soup, basmati encrusted scallops with leeks and lemon butter sauce, Alberta prime rib, oven roasted potato and Yorkshire pudding, finished with a chocolate terrine with lashings of raspberry coulis. But the final course is yet to come. Minuetta Kessler walks over to the piano. Quite delicately, she arranges herself on the bench, and as she had done in the 1930s, she captures the attention of an overly contented audience.

A signed photograph of Mrs. Kessler when she was a young concert pianist

*The original one-room cabins are built of peeled spruce; each cabin offers a personal retreat intended to reinforce the sense of mountain adventure. The simple interiors now feature private bathrooms.*

hangs in the balcony gallery. Pictures of artists Catharine and Peter Whyte and J.E.H. MacDonald, Tommy, Adeline and Margaret Link, Lawrence Grassi, George Harrison, Lester and Maxine Aaron, Sylvia Brewster Graves, and Phyllis and Austin Ford line the walls. Lake O'Hara Lodge was a favorite spot of Basil Gardom and his wife Gabrielle Gwladys. The guest ledgers read like a Who's Who of the Canadian Rockies: Major F.V. Longstaff, Georgia Engelhard, Edward Feuz, Charles Fay, Lillian Gest and hundreds of others who found pure joy here.

The fire crackles, the music fills the room and the spirits of those who made this place special seem to share in the moment. Another perfect day at Lake O'Hara Lodge comes to an end.

*The signature red roof of the most recent portion of Num-Ti-Jah Lodge is reflected in the willow flats of Bow Lake.*

# NUM-TI-JAH LODGE
## Banff National Park, Alberta

The small octagonal log cabin sits on a slight rise on the edge of Bow Lake. One hundred yards from the splendid Num-Ti-Jah Lodge, it usually goes unnoticed. The red shingles curl on the pyramid roof and a few windows of the enclosed verandah are cracked. But out of those panes unfolds one of the great views of the Canadian Rockies. A creek trickles through the willow flats and under a foot bridge, behind it the indigo blue of Bow Lake pours like spilled paint to an alpine skirt of evergreens. Crowfoot Mountain and tilting Saint Nicholas are to the southwest, and Portal Peak and Mount Thompson to the west. Saddled in the middle is the receding Bow Glacier, its falls dropping over limestone tiers to a landscape cut and crumbled by creeping ice.

At this spot, in 1898, young Jimmy Simpson vowed that one day he would "build a shack." That shack is The Ram Pasture, Simpson's one-time outfitting base and home. The quirky building eventually spawned the remarkable Num-Ti-Jah Lodge. The Ram Pasture and lodge are log and stone legacies of one of the great characters of Canada's Rockies.

Such a character that he's warranted a book on his life, dozens of interviews, a documentary and a retrospective at the Whyte Museum of the Canadian Rockies. A man who, at ninety, still held court in the Num-Ti-Jah lounge, telling tales as true or twisted as the high altitude pines of this place.

Simpson's life, as he liked to tell it, began in 1896 when he arrived in Canada from England. A mischievous and inquisitive nineteen-year-old, he quickly shed his family's plan to buy a farm, instead sweeping across Canada and the western United States in a youthful surge of exploration.

His remittance money long gone, Simpson landed in Banff and Lake Louise. Jimmy mixed with old timers of the Canadian Pacific Railroad, and was hired as a cook by pioneer outfitter Tom Wilson. He soon learned the ways of the trail, and for a kid who had never ridden a horse, he was a quick study.

That ability was probably the key to his fifty years of guiding success. Tourists of the era were wealthy and educated. Artists, botanists, doctors, teachers, authors and adventurers sought guides who not only knew how to pack a horse, but also were curious and could carry on bright conversations. Simpson became adept at both.

Over the next decade, Jimmy built up his business and his expertise as a guide and hunter. While the outdoors and all of its accouterments were the mainstay of his life, his interests were broad. He became fast friends with wildlife artist Carl Rungius and architect Walter Painter. He loved opera, and took up painting. Testimony of his self-taught penchant for architecture stands on the edge of Bow Lake.

Seemingly destined to the life of a rough and rugged bachelor, Jimmy sur-

CONSTRUCTED: 1922-24 (THE RAM PASTURE CABIN)
1937-39 (LODGE AND CABINS)
1948-56 (LODGE ADDITION)
BUILT BY: JAMES "JIMMY" SIMPSON

prised more than a few of his cohorts and married Williamina "Billie" Ross Reid in 1916. Jimmy was thirty-nine when their first child, Margaret, was born; Mary and Jimmy, Jr., followed. Jimmy's business ideas grew along with his family.

Unlike many lodges, the Simpson development at Bow Lake was not financed by a railway. The construction and operation of each phase was an affair between family and friends. Margaret and Mary grew up to be professional figure skaters; their earnings helped finance lodge construction. Jimmy, Jr., followed in his father's footsteps as an outfitter, guide and manager of Num-Ti-Jah Lodge.

Two decades after Jimmy vowed to "build a shack," he applied for land at the upper end of Bow Lake "for the erection of suitable buildings for tourist purposes." By September 1921, Simpson and parks reached an agreement: Jimmy could lease four acres on one of his favorite camp sites along Bow Lake for an annual rent of $40.

Even before the agreement was signed, Jimmy had gotten permission to begin work on the property. Running his outfitting operation, plus cutting timber, packing supplies twenty-six miles from Lake Louise station and building the camp proved more difficult than he anticipated. In the fall of 1922, Simpson requested an extension of his construction deadline. That extension was granted, but it wasn't until 1925 that Jimmy finally got a twenty-one-year lease. In the interim, he had spent the $5,000 required to secure a lease by building a log boat house, screened ga-

*Karl Hansen's final plans, dated February 1, 1939, for the lodge included the portion that was built beginning in 1937, right. The breezeway and addition to the left wouldn't begin for a decade; during that time, Jimmy Simpson's ideas for the lodge only expanded.*

zebo-like sleeping porch and a one-story octagonal cabin—The Ram Pasture.

Nothing between Simpson and parks went smoothly, and Jimmy seemed to find sport in sparring with bureaucrats. In 1929, when the parks accounting department decided that Simpson owed additional interest on overdue rental payments, his reply was classic Jimmy. "Regarding this interest dating back six years, some of it, is this a Head Office joke?…Please notify Head Office that I am not yet quite crazy or I will do it direct and do it real well if you would rather have me, but in the meantime, I am totally ignoring the matter," he wrote the parks superintendent.

Dominion Parks Commissioner J.B. Harkin, who knew Simpson and his contribution to parks tourism far better than any bean counter in "Head Office," waived the past due interest.

Commissioner Harkin believed that tourism was the key to the health of the national parks; it would be Harkin's vision of a road network through the parks that would impact Simpson far more than the nit-picking squabbles the department and Simpson engaged in.

Significant road work had been done during the 1920s, and while the initial funding for new roads was cut at the onset of the Depression, federally-funded work relief programs would be responsible for the construction of a spectacular new road between Lake Louise and Jasper that started in 1931. The Banff-Jasper Highway, as it came to be

known, would link the Canadian National Railways resort at Jasper with the CPR resorts at Lake Louise and Banff. More importantly for Simpson, the road would pass within a half mile of his camp, placing him at the crossroads of opportunity—an opportunity he had been preparing for since August 1924, when he mentioned the idea of a ten room structure for the site.

Jimmy's grand plans were always evolving, and in 1937 Simpson, Vern Castella, who had done the log work on The Ram Pasture, and carpenter Karl Hansen—along with the Simpson clan—began turning Jimmy's lodge vision into reality. By that time, Margaret and Mary's skating careers were

*The 1940 Num-Ti-Jah Lodge played upon the octagonal shape of The Ram Pasture. The original entrance, right, is now the gift shop.*

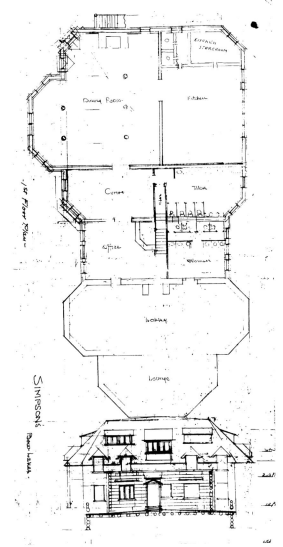

successful enough for the girls to finance the building.

Road construction provided rock and road access to a burn area near Mistaya Lake where long timbers were obtained. What Jimmy failed to provide were plans, drawings or building permits before he started building. Simpson was a friend of architect Walter Painter, designer of the additions for Chateau Lake Louise and Banff Springs Hotel among other assignments. On July 3, 1938, Simpson wrote Superintendent P.J. Jennings: "...Mr. Walter Painter has not yet sent in plans as promised. Just to conform with the regulations as required would you send up one of your staff architects at my expense sometime next week and let him make plans from what is now constructed under my informational direction. I will supply him his noonday oats and undoubtedly he would like to be away from you all for a day."

On September 19, 1938, Jennings wrote Jimmy the obvious: construction work at Bow Lake was being done without plans or permit. The superintendent outlined regulations Simpson knew of but chose to ignore. Since the crew already was working on the thirty-seven-by-fifty-foot structure, a bit of good news came to Simpson's attention. His finish carpenter, Karl Hansen, had some drafting experience. With Simpson pushing to use every minute of good weather for construction, he shot off a reply: "My architect, Mr. Carl Hansen of Calgary, who is at present on

location will prepare a complete set of plans with out buildings such as electric light building or power house, and will add the present construction to the plans so that the Department can see what is proposed and also being done."

No plans followed and Jennings sent him a reminder on October 28. Two days later, Simpson wrote Jennings: "I have yours of the 28th instant. In reply I beg to state that I have this day seen my architect Mr. Carl Hansen of Calgary, who is at present in Banff, relative to the above.

"Mr. Hansen, not thinking there was any hurry in this matter, left they [*sic*] in abeyance and busied himself with plans of Sir Norman Watson's structure in the Ptarmigan Valley. He has, however, assured me he will get at them as soon as he returns to his drafting board in Calgary, but in the meantime he has left a rough drawing in my hands so that I can assure your office he is engaged on this. His drawing I will show you tomorrow.

"I am writing this so that you will have the matter on file and can so state to Head Office.

"Thanking you for your courtesy and apologising for the delay which causes your office extra correspondence."

Simpson did indeed show a pencil sketch of the proposed buildings to the superintendent, who was no doubt tiring of the entire affair. Jennings found the sketch satisfactory, but that was not the case at parks headquarters in Ottawa. Two weeks later, Jennings advised Simpson that work on the buildings at Bow Lake must cease until plans were submitted for departmental approval and building permits were issued.

Simpson sent still incomplete plans drawn by Hansen to Jennings on November 16. On December 14, Jennings, ready for a holiday respite, issued a building permit. The final plans, signed by Karl Hansen and dated February 1, 1939, did not land on Jennings' desk until February 7. Those drawings included Simpson's complete vision—a

*Jimmy Simpson built the three-tiered fireplace in the lounge/library now flanked by chairs crafted for Mary Schäffer, one of the Canadian Rockies' early women explorers.*

The waiting room, left, outside of the dining room.

Num-Ti-Jah Lodge is a monument to Jimmy Simpson as is the peak
named after him that can be seen from the lodge, below.

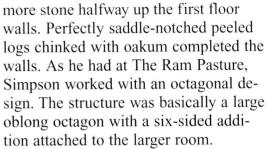

vision not finished until the 1950s.

While paperwork was flying, a rock and timber lodge like nothing the "backcountry" had seen had gone up. With access to almost unlimited rock from the highway construction, Simpson chose to build the lodge on stone footings with a stone foundation and

more stone halfway up the first floor walls. Perfectly saddle-notched peeled logs chinked with oakum completed the walls. As he had at The Ram Pasture, Simpson worked with an octagonal design. The structure was basically a large oblong octagon with a six-sided addition attached to the larger room.

The second story is supported by peeled joist beams held by interior posts and beams. The log work is marvelous, especially on the ceiling where a series of short spoke beams connect to the main beams and extend to the exterior to support the eaves and roof.

As the walls went up, the question of what kind of roof could top the building was the puzzle of the day. Pieces to that particular puzzle came together as a steeply pitched roof with three main gables, each with deep overhangs and eaves off the first floor. Thirteen valleys and various pitches follow the corner joints, a plan meant to let the snow slide off the roof. Four dormer windows run along the back wall and the original entrance (now the gift shop) faces southeast. The original roof was covered with cedar shingles. Upstairs, six bedrooms and two bathrooms were readied for guests who could also stay in the various cabins on the property.

As a finishing exterior touch, Simpson imbedded his collection of crystals along the stone ledge on the perimeter of the building. Rock collectors too lazy to hunt for their own specimens have chiseled out a few of the crystals. In the

days when Jimmy was alive, a club-wielding Simpson would chase them off the property.

Inside, wood sheeting covers the lower cement work and split logs trim the beautiful casement windows. Simpson was an avid collector of wildlife and wilderness art that included pieces by friend Carl Rungius. These, along with family photographs, Jimmy's watercolors and various hunting trophies, gave the lodge a homey atmosphere.

Simpson built the three-tiered stone fireplace that anchors the larger room, originally used as the dining room, now the main lounge library. When asked if such a huge fireplace could possibly draw, Jimmy retorted, "It'll draw the socks off your feet!"

Furniture was acquired over time. Oversized Arts & Crafts style tables, chairs, writing desks and a daybed, bought from Dave White & Co. in Banff, now fill the main lounge library. A desk and a few wooden chairs belonged to A.O. Wheeler, interprovincial surveyor and first president of the Alpine Club of Canada. But the signature pieces are two chairs that flank the fireplace. A moose rack and set of elk antlers form the back and arms of the chairs built for Mary Schäffer, one of the Canadian Rockies' early women explorers.

Guests had been staying at the camp each season during construction. Until the kitchen took shape, Billie cooked from a tent for guests who were making their way up the unfinished road from Lake Louise to Bow Lake.

When the Banff-Jasper Highway officially opened in 1940, Simpson's Num-Ti-Jah Lodge (named after the Stoney Indian word for pine marten and originally spelled Num-Ti-Gah), was complete—at least for a while.

Even with parks permit, policy and payment problems, the lodge was a going concern. The Simpson girls were making a name for themselves in professional ice skating; Jimmy, Jr., could guide and hunt with the best; and Billie and Jimmy might now reap some benefits from years of grueling work. But World War II and a family tragedy changed that. Rationing of tires and gasoline implemented in 1942 left Num-Ti-Jah Lodge virtually empty, but not as empty as the void left by the unexpected death of eldest daughter Margaret. In 1941, Margaret Simpson Brown died from complications of pregnancy.

By 1942, Jimmy, Jr., had enlisted in the Air Force and, grappling with their grief and economic hardships, the Simpsons continued dividing their time between their home in Banff and Num-Ti-Jah. In January of that year, Jimmy reported to Jennings that he had spent approximately $22,000 on a modern chalet and outbuildings when he applied for an extension of ten acres for corrals and to protect his water supply. A much tempered Jimmy negotiated and signed a twenty-one-year lease renewal on April 2, 1943—post-dated Sept. 1, 1942—for 4.76 acres.

Jimmy knew that after the war tourism would return and his family's future would rely on lodge profits. His vision for expansion was on paper in Hansen's plans, but in his mind, the project was already growing. But he would need funding.

The Simpsons' Banff home was next door to Catharine and Peter Whyte's home and studio. The couple stayed with the Simpsons when they painted at Bow Lake. They had financed construction at Skoki Lodge, and with funds available and years of friendship, Catharine Whyte made the loan.

The amount of the loan Jimmy quoted in later correspondence to Superintendent Hutchinson was $50,000. With financing in place, in 1948, Jimmy, Jr., hired Ken Jones to head the construction crew. Jones had done the log work at Skoki Lodge, and he was a well-known mountain guide, decent cook, and a tenacious worker.

Of course, there were no plans. "I asked him for plans like you're supposed to do," explained Jones of his conversation with Jimmy. "He said, 'Come on, I'll show you the plans.' He heads down to the sandbar. He sticks a stick in the sand, and [Jimmy said] 'It goes this way, this way, and that way and that way, and this way, and around and around.' 'I'd like to have the blueprints,' I said. 'Oh, hell with the blue-

*Nashan Lounge was created as a billiard and trophy room.*

how the building was going to go up, his father replied: "It goes up up up with a roof on it." And that's what happened.

From the foundation, everything went up one log at a time. The logs were run up on skids, centered, measured then turned over to chisel the half-circle notches. They were then put in place, held with draft pins at eight foot intervals and chinked with ship-grade oakum, a creosote treated rope.

"If the government ever tried to pull it down, they'd have to try to burn it down or saw it down," related Simpson in a 1971 interview. "This fellow Jones did a first class job."

The log work progressed until snow halted construction. By then, only half of the first floor's log work had been completed. The lodge was going up with no plans yet submitted to parks. Superintendent James Hutchinson would have the pleasure of taking over where Jennings had left off.

In February 1949, Jimmy sent the superintendent plans for a four-story log lodge drawn by his friend Walter Painter. Unfortunately, Jimmy did not like Painter's drawings, and outlined changes point by point.

Instead of a four-story log building with a moderately pitched gable roof lined with traditional dormers, Jimmy wanted logs to end after the first floor with frame construction above that. He added a kitchen storeroom and washrooms, eliminated a balcony, lopped off

prints, you can put it up!'"

Jones borrowed graph paper from Mary Simpson and sketched out his own plans according to "old Jim's" wishes. Logs were hauled from the burn area at Silverhorn Creek, but the eighty-foot trees needed to span the seventy-six-foot long main walls were hand-picked from around Hector Lake. Once moved to Bow Lake, they were set aside to dry.

In the meantime, Jimmy and his brother-in-law Bill Stewart had been hand building the rock and cement foundation. The foundation and four-

foot-high walls had rockwork facia built against concrete, creating a two-foot-thick base for what would eventually be a two-story building plus attic accommodations. Jimmy, Jr., Jones and other crew members spent the first month cutting and trucking logs.

"So, I started working on the stone foundation to find the ninety and forty-five degree angles, but the old man never measured them....It's symmetrical in principle; in the technical part, I don't think there are two angles that are alike," recalled Jones.

When Jimmy, Jr., asked his father

one story, made a steeper roof and changed the half-cut cantilevered log design.

"In this stone and concrete age a building of log construction is not within the orbit of a modern architect and one has to use their own discretion in relation to many matters," Simpson wrote Hutchinson in obvious reference to Painter's concrete wing at Chateau Lake Louise and stone tower at the Banff Springs Hotel. "I can hardly tell Mr. Painter he is wrong so must ask the Department to give heed to the remarks I have stressed when they diagnose the drawings and make their decision…"

Hutchinson agreed with Simpson's astute assessment of the plans and forwarded them with his recommendation to Ottawa where they got a stamp of approval, and a building permit for a $30,000 structure was issued the following November. When spring came, it was back to going up, up, up one log at a time.

Jones and Jimmy, Jr., came in early spring, shoveled the snow off the logs and peeled them so they would dry. The rounds of log work began. At the end of the room Jimmy built a massive stone fireplace, and as the logs went up so did the fireplace.

The most difficult log work was fitting the new structure to the original building. Jones and his crew would carefully chisel double notches at joining corners and fit the logs through the existing wall with one man working at

*The Ram Pasture was the original camp building and home of Jimmy Simpson. It set the tone for the eclectic lodge that stands today.*

*The Num-Ti-Jah addition created the dining room with its soaring eighteen-foot-high ceilings, stone fireplace and adjoining kitchen on the first floor.*

progressed above the first story windows—windows that Simpson had personally designed. It was at this point where the eighty-foot logs were placed. The dining room has sixteen-foot ceilings; single and double beams span the room supported by posts, some made of four upright timbers.

It was obvious that the lodge couldn't be finished that year. Jimmy wanted it enclosed with a roof before winter, so a crew of carpenters was hired to frame the building and figure out how to "put a roof on it."

By October, the lodge was enclosed and topped by a roof whose construction was as challenging as predicted. Each rafter had to be hoisted, measured and marked, then lowered and beveled, then hoisted again. The roofline is a jagged maze of hips, valleys and fourteen dormers, a fitting reflection of the surrounding Rocky Mountain peaks.

Jimmy wrote Superintendent Hutchinson on October 18, 1949 that everything had been sheeted in and the shingling was half completed. Twenty-two new rooms were laid out, with a suite for Jimmy, Jr., and his new wife, Lorna Oliver, on the second floor, but the lodge would not be ready for the July 1, 1950 opening. Instead, Jimmy thought that the first floor of ten rooms would be finished. Friends and family arrived for the grand opening, and seeing the carpenters still at work, they pitched in, moving everything from the cast iron stove to furniture into place.

"Big Jim was so pleased to see his dream coming true that he just stood and watched and every once in a while would let out a real laugh and slap someone on the back," Catharine Whyte wrote her mother following the party.

At the end of the 1950 season, construction resumed and continued until snow closed it down. Jimmy incorporated the operation in 1952 to Num-Ti-Jah Lodge Ltd. Jimmy and Billie spent their summers living in The Ram Pasture, returning to their Banff home for the winter. Jimmy, Jr., took over lodge operation and continued with improvements; his sister Mary spent her summers working at the lodge.

Num-Ti-Jah Lodge was finished in 1954 when steam heat was added. By 1956, accommodations included the main lodge, The Ram Pasture and three cabins to sleep seventy guests. Besides room for lodgers, the compound had a laundry building, water tower, power house and a fire equipment shed. The laundry building burned in 1990, and the water tower was dismantled in the late 1950s, but the power house stands and the fire shed is now a cedar-lined dry sauna. Since packing was still a going concern, there were also a corral and saddle shed. A bunk house was dismantled in Banff and moved to Num-Ti-Jah in 1956 to house the wranglers.

The signature red roof was added in 1950. Num-Ti-Jah opened for its first winter season in 1963. "Dad wouldn't come up that winter, but when he found

out that we didn't all freeze to death, he came up," recalled Jimmy, Jr.

A seasonal ski lift was planned, but government permission was withdrawn and Jimmy, Jr., turned to snowmobiling to draw tourists. Today, cross-country skiers and snowshoers head out from the lodge, and downhill enthusiasts travel to nearby resorts.

The elder Simpsons made their year round home at The Ram Pasture in 1968. Billie Simpson died that year at the age of 77. Jimmy remained in the little octagonal cabin where it all began, where he read, painted and kept up correspondence and civic responsibilities as a pioneer of the Rockies. Jimmy carried on as the patriarch of Num-Ti-Jah Lodge until October 30, 1972, when he passed away at the age of 95. Two years later, the legend of the Rockies was honored by the naming of Mount Jimmy Simpson that can be seen from the lodge.

Num-Ti-Jah Lodge does not have the permanence of a mountain peak, but it too is a monument to the man and his family. The battles and bravado, the pranks and passion are all there in timber and stone topped by the red roofs forming a continuing confluence of ridges and valleys.

"It's all up here," Simpson used to say of his Num-Ti-Jah plans, as he pointed under his flat-brimmed Stetson hat. "It's all up here."

*Num-Ti-Jah's peaks, valleys and dormers define its silhouette against the dull whiteness of a winter day.*

# The Backcountry

THE BACKCOUNTRY EXPERIENCE OFFERS
ITS OWN SIMPLE LUXURIES: A HEARTY MEAL SERVED IN
HEAPING PORTIONS, ROOMS CAUGHT IN THE GLOW OF KEROSENE OR
CANDLE LIGHT, WARM BEDS AND THE CAMERADERIE SHARED BY
STRANGERS. TWIN FALLS CHALET, ABBOT PASS HUT, SKOKI, MOUNT
ASSINIBOINE AND SHADOW LAKE LODGES ARE ALL IN REMOTE AND
SPECTACULAR SETTINGS, AND GUESTS ARE STILL REQUIRED TO
WORK—IN VARYING DEGREES—TO GET TO THESE SURVIVING
RETREATS. FOR THOSE WILLING TO TRAIPSE BACK IN TIME,
THEY ARE THERE FOR THE EXPERIENCE.

# TWIN FALLS CHALET

The five-mile trail along the Yoho River from Takakkaw Falls trailhead to Twin Falls Chalet is one of the most traveled in Yoho National Park, yet hikers seem few and far between. The river is caught and released again and again creating Angel's Staircase, Point Lace, and then Laughing falls. Twin Falls is the grand finale, an aquatic fit of activity that culminates off the limestone ledge that splits the melt from Glacier des Poilus into two tongues of frothing foam dropping  264 feet. One hundred yards from the base of the falls is Twin Falls Chalet.

It is obvious that those who select the parks' trail signs aren't concerned if anyone finds the chalet. Hikers seem to stumble upon it, and they stop for homemade soup, freshly baked pastries or afternoon tea. Most move on. There is the famous "Attention: Before asking any questions, check to see if any of these answers will fit..." sign posted on the door, not exactly a welcome, how-do-you-do. But for those who made reservations and stay over, there awaits the unexpected. The Twin Falls experience is like no other.

Peeking through the forest between the trail junction and the falls basin is a

line of billowing laundry. The flapping sheets and towels hanging from the chalet's balcony to a tree are getting a final rinse from mother nature. Their dull thump, and a low rumble from the falls, are the only sounds.

The building itself seems part of the forest: massive locally harvested logs

are laid horizontally creating a charming and much weathered shelter. Except for a row of white folding chairs, the chalet today appears virtually identical to its photographs taken in the 1930s. And its looks are not deceiving.

There are no running water, no plumbing, no electricity at Twin Falls Chalet. Meals are cooked on a wood burning stove, outhouses come with

views, and the dark recesses of the low-ceilinged lounge and dining area are lighted by kerosene lamps. Water is fetched in pails from the glacial runoff for cooking, cleaning and laundry, and supplies arrive by pack horse.

Inside, the staff is cleaning blueberries for the night's salad. Innkeeper Fran Drummond looks up from her work, a smile stretches across her face, and she wipes her hand on her apron and sticks it out for a bracing welcome. The fun is about to begin, and it has been this way for almost forty years, since Fran started running the place.

"I hope you aren't disappointed," she says as she turns back to her cooking. The room is filled with a light haze of smoke. The kitchen's open shelves are lined with colorful bowls, pitchers and teapots. Every inch of the stove holds a steaming pot of something. An intoxicating aroma of smoke, lemon oil and simmering food fills the room. The three women working here don't miss a beat, and a pot of tea is set on the kitchen table. I plop down sure that absolutely nothing could be disappointing about this place.

**CONSTRUCTED: 1908 (ORIGINAL CABIN); 1917 (ADDITION)**
**1923 (MAIN TEA HOUSE)**
**BUILT BY: CANADIAN PACIFIC RAILWAY**

*Little has changed at Twin Falls Chalet since the 1946 photo, left, or when John Murray Gibbon, the CPR's ace publicity agent, above, made notes on the chalet's verandah. Gibbon was as much at home promoting the backcountry as the company's international tours.*

"The cowboys who were supposed to haul in the food got drunk at the Stampede and things sat there for three days and got rotten and had to be thrown out," explains Fran. "There's one disaster every season, and I guess that was it."

I'm happy to hear that, since I'm also told that tomorrow ten loads of fire wood will be dropped by helicopter next to the chalet.

Helicopters seem quite a contrast to the pristine setting, but aerial drops of wood have been used since 1994 when Yoho National Park implemented "non-

impact" use of local firewood for all backcountry facilities. Yoho is the smallest of the Canadian Rocky Mountain National Parks, and Yoho Valley is in the northern reaches of the park.

The area was explored in 1897 by a member of the German Austrian Alpine Club, professor Jean Habel. He crossed Yoho Pass, discovered Takakkaw Falls and wrote about the Yoho Glacier. But the alluvial fields, lush valley, and cascading series of glacial waterfalls got international recognition in 1901 when the Canadian Pacific Railway hosted Edward Whymper, who had become

synonymous with mountaineering when he made the first—albeit tragic—ascent of the Matterhorn in 1865. The CPR hoped that Whymper, then sixty-one, would tackle some of the unconquered peaks—most notably Mount Assiniboine—and write a book about his exploits. Instead, Whymper enjoyed the largess of the CPR, and with a full entourage, explored much of the region including the Yoho Valley.

Alpinists and the publicity department of the CPR may have been disappointed, but local climbers and outfitters knew of the extraordinary charms

*The first portion of the chalet was the cabin, far right, constructed in 1908. The center addition came in 1917, and the two-story chalet was built six years later as part of the railway's backcountry development.*

of the Yoho Valley. The trail from Takakkaw Falls to Twin Falls had been cleared by the CPR at the turn of the century, and the railway and Alpine Club of Canada continued to create a trail system through Yoho Valley.

Surveyors and outfitters needed shelter and, about 1908, the first portion of what is now Twin Falls Chalet was built of locally cut and peeled logs. The logs are joined with double-notched corners

and chinked with oakum, a creosote treated rope.

The surveyors or outfitters who likely built the shelter fully appreciated what was out their front door. Instead of the usual small windows of like structures, the two windows flanking the entry are nearly the full height of the one-story cabin. The double vision of Twin Falls was as astounding then as it has been for the decades since. The large win-

dows and doorway are framed by split unpeeled logs and the cabin is topped with a pitched, cedar-shingled roof. In 1917, a small addition, also built of local but consistently smaller logs, was added to the original cabin. (That addition now links the original cabin to the two-story chalet.)

The 1920s expansion of CPR facilities included enlarging its hotels, building and upgrading bungalow camps, and creating tea houses and rest houses along the expanding network of roads and trails. Each hotel, each camp, each tea house, each trail defined the mountain experience mapped out by the railway. Twin Falls Chalet was one of the picturesque tea houses built along the trails that offered respite, meals and, in some instances, accommodations to riders and alpinists reveling in the Rocky Mountain experience.

In October 1922, the CPR's Basil Gardom requested permission to construct a "rest camp" at Twin Falls as an addition to the cabin, and permission to cut the necessary timber for its construction. Parks Superintendent E.W. Russell endorsed the request, and forwarded the application on to J.B. Harkin, Commissioner of Dominion Parks in Ottawa. A permit was issued in August 1923 to construct a tea house and rest house of peeled logs with an estimated value of $1,500.

A crew with Bert McCorkle as foreman constructed the tea house under the direction of Gardom. Axemen included George Harrison, a Banff outfitter, who would later be the foreman for construction of Lake O'Hara Lodge.

Rather than duplicate the cabin style, the building took on what the railway found appropriate mountain architecture with a Swiss chalet design. It was attached to the cabin addition and the joinery work illustrates the crew's axemanship. Again, massive locally harvested trees were used for construction

*Helicopters now deliver wood to backcountry lodges and cabins in Yoho National Park.*

with squared double-notched corners.

Traditionally, logs of this size are reserved for larger structures where they emphasize the enormity of a soaring great hall or to make a statement about the importance of a structure. If log size was the gauge, Twin Falls Chalet would be the most significant building in the CPR's hotel empire. Instead, the trees stack up to create a simple twenty-two-by-twenty-two, two-story building with a deep overhang that shelters a second floor balcony. The balcony and overhang are supported by two large peeled timber columns, and a thirty-foot log holds the balcony between the columns. The railing is a simple log design; split and peeled logs frame the windows and doors both inside and out.

By October, Twin Falls rest house was ready for business, and the CPR applied for a twenty-one-year lease for one acre around the site. Approval of one-half acre for $10 per year was granted, satisfying both parties.

The publicity department of the railway produced a barrage of brochures overloaded with understandably flowery prose. In 1927, the *Bungalow Camps of the Canadian Pacific Rockies* booklet included "The Tea House": "For the majority the ride up the valley to the culminating glacier is enough for one day. One does not wish to glut the mind, does not wish to pack over-summarily into the store-house of memory too much beauty all at once. That ride from camp to where the trails fork can well be taken again without growing weary of it. But one does not…have to return at once, for close to the Twin Falls is Twin Falls Tea House, a picturesque log-cabin house that provides meals that would be attractive anywhere, but are…more highly appreciated because they are where they are, and also have sleeping accommodation."

The railway continued to operate the Twin Falls Tea House, and in December 1943, reported to parks a $4,194 capital investment in the property with a $2,728.93 deficit after depreciation (but before interest on investment). The railway renewed its lease in 1944.

By September 1953, the CPR's hotel system had "disposed" of its mountain lodges at Castle Mountain and Radium

*When the crashing water of Twin Falls seemed to favor one side more than the other, the CPR used a little dynamite to insure that the falls would indeed be twins.*

Hot Springs. As a company representative explained: "Mountain Lodges at Lake Wapta and Yoho Valley were originally constructed in 1921 and 1906 respectively, for the purpose of encouraging a certain class of traffic to visit the Canadian Rockies by train and were designed to provide modest accommodation for those who either preferred a more rustic atmosphere or could not afford the more pretentious resorts at Banff and Lake Louise."

The lodges had served their purposes, but after World War II, the memo continued, "the growing popularity of motor travel, better highways and larger numbers of automobiles" had drastically changed the destinations. When it was time to divest themselves of the larger properties, the company no longer wished "to continue the operation of the Twin Falls Tea House, which would be included with the Yoho Valley Lodge if and when the property was sold."

In March 1954, the railway's hotel division indeed entered into agreement to sell its Yoho interests excluding Emerald Lake Chalet to Brewster and Ford Mountain Lodges Limited. The buildings to be sold were Lake O'Hara Lodge, Wapta Lodge, Yoho Valley Lodge and Twin Falls Tea House. (The Tea House had been closed to the public since 1953.) Emerald Lake Chalet was sold in 1959, and the Lake Wapta Camp and Yoho Valley Camp were later dismantled. Twin Falls reopened and Lake O'Hara Lodge continues operating in

*The chalet was built so guests could get a full view of the falls from the second floor balcony.*

much the same fashion as it did as a deluxe bungalow camp.

In 1962, Fran Drummond became proprietor of the tea house. Drummond was raised in Mexico and had traveled extensively "but was a mountain girl since I was fifteen!" She had worked at other backcountry lodges in the Canadian Rockies, but Twin Falls Chalet became her passion.

In 1969, Parks Canada made an egregious error in judgment. They recommended the demolition of Twin Falls Tea House noting that the structure was in poor repair. The report also stated that water had to be carried from the stream by hand, light was by coal oil or other gas lamps, heat by wood stoves, and toilet facilities were dry privies outside of the main building.

Some things should never change. Drummond had no intention that her "labor of love, not a darn thing more" was going to be wasted. She mounted a letter writing campaign to her clients and with the support of the press, they derailed demolition plans. Today, the chalet is a National Historic Site.

Some renovation and repairs took place in 1970, and two years later Drummond renewed the parks' lease in her name. Bark was peeled from the interior kitchen and storeroom walls, and floors were scrubbed down to bare wood with a steel brush. A new cedar roof and skylights over the kitchen were added in 1979-80. A custom built gas-motored washing machine was delivered by helicopter and, at the parks' insistence, a water filtration system was added in 1995-96 for kitchen and laundry gray water. It still takes twelve pails of stream water per laundry load, and there are four loads of sheets and towels each day. A kitchen sink replaced two dish pans, but water is still hauled, heated and poured for washing and cleaning.

The guest rooms have always been snug and rustic. Instead of the original metal-framed CPR beds (they hang rusting from the back of the chalet), wooden bunk beds with firm mattresses and sheet-lined down sleeping bags keep guests warm on chilly nights. Small battery powered lanterns are the only light, and Fran hands out torches for late night trips to the privy. A metal bowl and pitcher sit on a stand for washing.

Multi-course, hearty meals are miraculously prepared and brought to a long dining room table situated in the main lounge. The room is dark even in midday, and the kerosene lamps offer a soft light. Bowls and platters of chicken, rice, fresh vegetables and salad arrive, and if guests don't fill each chair, Fran and her assistants join everyone for dinner. It is like a family reunion with long lost aunts and cousins exchanging stories of the day.

After dinner, guests make their way upstairs and climb into the tiny bunks.

"The next thing we knew it was morning; smell of wood smoke, coffee, and frying bacon awakened us to fresh adventures," wrote Gordon Brinley in *Away in the Canadian Rockies*, published in 1938. That is exactly how my morning begins.

I make my way to the kitchen, and get a cup of coffee. I am barely awake

*Guest rooms are snug and simple.*

when Fran serenades me with "My Little Yoho Lady." I should be drunk to yodel with her, but I'm not, and I sing anyway.

There is another delicious meal, then everyone sets off for their hike of the day. We follow Whaleback Trail to the crest of Twin Falls. The narrow path of switchbacks takes about an hour. A fifteen-foot cable bridge spans the milky river of melted glacier water. We gingerly step to the ledge and gaze at a whirlpool that pounds against the giant bowl of rock bellowing its last hurrah before hurling through a tunnel and plummeting below. Clouds roll across the scene then there is a short burst of showers. A spiral of smoke can be seen below, and there is a speck in the clearing—tiny Twin Falls Chalet.

We hike back and I fetch a mug of steaming tea and a hot homemade butter tart, and I settle on the balcony. The sun breaks through the cloud cover and blue sky colors the gray that is then cut by the arch of a triple rainbow. The tart melts in my mouth, the tea warms me. I stare up at the little ledge where only an hour ago I was standing, and my eyes ever-so-slowly follow the falls.

Suddenly, my trance is broken by the roar of a helicopter, whose noise signals, "Action"! Fran bursts from the kitchen and rushes to the woodshed a few yards away. Her arms wave the pilot into position, the blades churn a torrent of wind. The hanging laundry is blown parallel to the ground. A hook is released and the first bounty of firewood drops from its yellow webbed sling. After a moment of stunned silence, staff and guests run to stack the logs and the scene is repeated.

As the helicopter swoops away and the final logs are stacked there is the familiar sound of the low rumble of Twin Falls.

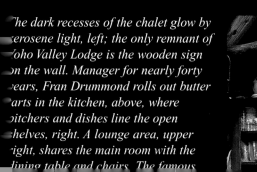

The dark recesses of the chalet glow by kerosene light, left; the only remnant of Yoho Valley Lodge is the wooden sign on the wall. Manager for nearly forty years, Fran Drummond rolls out butter tarts in the kitchen, above, where pitchers and dishes line the open shelves, right. A lounge area, upper right, shares the main room with the dining table and chairs. The famous

Chateau Lake Louise had long been a launch point for mountaineers tackling the peaks, icefields and glaciers along the Continental Divide. Climbs of Mount Victoria and Mount Lefroy were gaining popularity in the early 1920s, and Swiss guides Edward Feuz and Rudolph Aemmer suggested to Basil Gardom that the Canadian Pacific Railway build a hut as a base camp for mountaineers on those long ascents. Gardom, who had climbed with Feuz, Aemmer and other guides, convinced CPR executives to endorse the project.

Unlike other rest houses, this would not be on a wooded trail like Twin Falls Chalet or set in an alpine meadow like Lake O'Hara Camp. Instead, Abbot Hut is perched on a 9,589-foot promontory on Abbot Pass straddling the Divide. The hut does not offer traditional lodge accommodations, but it is a unique example of high altitude architecture and construction.

It is a simple, stone structure—a rectangular box—with a complicated story.

That story begins with the pass and hut's namesake, Philip Stanley Abbot. An experienced and popular climber from Boston and a member of the Ap-

palachian Mountain Club of Boston, Abbot was with a party attempting their second ascent of Mount Lefroy on August 3, 1896. As his friends watched, Abbot, only seconds before in perfect control, tumbled backwards and plunged 1,000 feet. Three climbers needed three hours to reach Abbot, who

was still clinging to life. He died during the subsequent descent, and it would be days before his body was recovered from where his climbing partners left him.

The accident, North America's first mountaineering fatality, caused a media stir that challenged the very idea of the sport. While members of Abbot's party dealt with their grief, they in turn wanted to validate their loss by proving that Mount Lefroy was climbable. A party made up of renowned climbers of the day including members of the Appalachian Mountain Club, with Charles Fay who had been on the fatal climb, and Professor Harold Baily Dixon, Fellow of the Royal Society and member of the Alpine Club, and led by professional Swiss guide Peter Sarbach, made plans to ascend the peak. A year after Philip Abbot's death, the party made the first ascent of Mount Lefroy and two days later made the first ascent of Mount Victoria.

It would take until 1898, but that year the CPR signed contracts with two Swiss guides, Edward Feuz, Sr., and Christian Häsler, Sr., to lead climbers up the peaks of the Canadian Rockies.

Two decades later, Swiss guides would construct Abbot Hut, in many ways more challenging than ascending the peaks. Feuz took charge of the arduous task. Two tons of cement, lime, bolts, windows, timbers, furnishings and supplies had to be transported to the site. Materials were first taken by raft across Lake Louise then packed on

**OPENED: Spring 1923 (Abbot Pass Hut)**
**NATIONAL HISTORIC SITE**
**OPENED: 1924 (Plain of Six Glaciers Tea House)**
**BUILT BY: Canadian Pacific Railway**

123

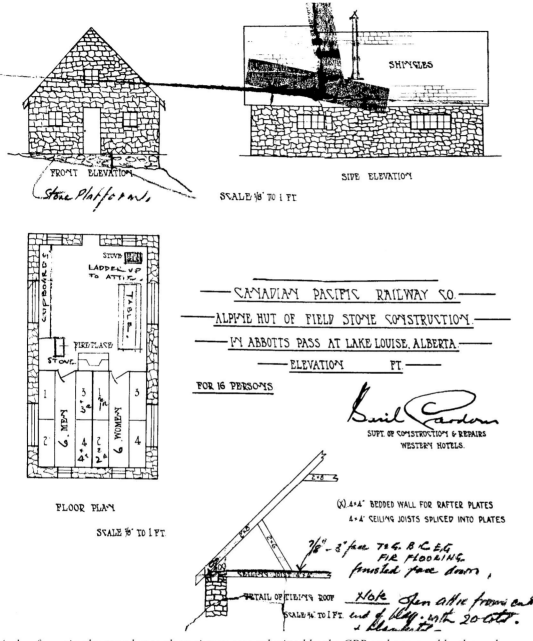

FRONT ELEVATION

Stone Platform,

SCALE 1/8" TO 1 FT

SIDE ELEVATION

SHINGLES

FLOOR PLAN

STOVE

CUPBOARD

LADDER UP TO ATTIC

TABLE

FIREPLACE

STOVE

1  3  1+3+2  3

2  4  2+4  4

♂ MEN    ♀ WOMEN

SCALE 1/8" TO 1 FT.

CANADIAN PACIFIC RAILWAY CO.

ALPINE HUT OF FIELD STONE CONSTRUCTION.

IN ABBOTTS PASS AT LAKE LOUISE, ALBERTA.

ELEVATION        FT.

FOR 16 PERSONS

SUPT. OF CONSTRUCTION & REPAIRS
WESTERN HOTELS.

(X) 4×4" BEDDED WALL FOR RAFTER PLATES
4×4" CEILING JOISTS SPLICED INTO PLATES

DETAIL OF TIE-IN ROOF

SCALE 1/4" TO 1 FT.

*A plan for a simple stone hut to sleep sixteen was submitted by the CPR and approved by the parks department for use as a base camp for mountaineers.*

horses. Where horses could not maneuver the icy terrain or cross the treacherous crevasses, supplies were hoisted by Swiss guides over a series of ladders with winches.

Built of split stone, with a medium-pitch gable roof, the hut was fastened to the bedrock with cables defying the winds that roared over the site. Completed in 1922, the hut officially opened in the spring of 1923 with basic sleeping and cooking accommodations for thirty.

By the 1960s, the hut had fallen into disrepair. The CPR wanted to give it to the Alpine Club of Canada, who declined responsibility. In 1968 the stone shelter came under the jurisdiction of National and Historic Parks Branch. At that point, the hut's roof leaked and portions were missing, the floor boards and entry door were broken, and the structure was littered with trash and rat-eaten mattresses. Local skiers and mountaineers volunteered to work on restoration, and Parks Canada allocated $5,000 to the cause.

Volunteers cleaned, painted, and hauled away garbage. Park carpenters put in a new fir floor, insulated the upper area and paneled the building. The exterior was chinked and the paper-thin roof reshingled.

Today, the humble stone building with its complex story is a National Historic Site—the highest such in Canada. Climbers still follow the route from Chateau Lake Louise past the Plain of Six Glaciers Tea House via Victoria Glacier and up aptly named "Death Trap," or head to the pass on the route from Lake O'Hara. Ascent to the pass from Lake Louise is very difficult—more so today due to glacial recession—and should be attempted only by experienced and fully equipped mountaineeers or with a guide. Access from Lake O'Hara is not technical, but is a long, grueling scramble up steep, loose rock from Lake Oesa, and it can be dangerous when there is fresh snow.

The Alpine Club of Canada manages

the hut and dedicated climbers find respite there from the howling winds of Abbot Pass.

The tiny Plain of Six Glaciers Tea House nestled off the trail from Chateau Lake Louise to Abbot Pass looks like it was plucked from the Swiss Alps. And for good reason. The two-story, stone chalet was built by the CPR, and like Abbot Pass Hut, the idea of a shelter along the popular climbing route came from a Swiss guide, Edward Feuz.

The CPR submitted plans for the tea house in January 1924, and after a few revisions, the company obtained a building permit a month later. The tea house would be on a parcel of land a little more than three miles from Chateau Lake Louise on a rough trail that began on the north shore of the lake. Sandstone was quarried from nearby, timbers cut and peeled and additional building supplies carried by pack horse from the Lake Louise Station to the site.

The chalet plans, signed by Gardom, called for a "Swiss chalet to be used by mountaineers." The chalet plans are for a stone structure, the same material as Abbot Pass Hut, with a steeply pitched roof and deep eaves to cover a wrap-around balcony. The first floor was for a tea room, kitchen, and bedroom with two exterior stairways to additional upstairs bedrooms. A back room shown on the plans was never constructed.

The entire tea house, including the porch, was built on a stone foundation. Peeled log timbers hold the front balcony

*Swiss guides Rudolf Aemmer, Edward Feuz and Val Flynn pose on a pinnacle on Abbot Pass along with CPR's Basil Gardom, right. The stone hut, below, was built by the Swiss guides who suggested the project to Gardom as part of the company's backcountry development, circa 1930.*

Plain of Six Glaciers Tea House, on the trail from Lake Louise, still serves tea and lunch to hikers.

with peeled log railings and balustrades. Inside, a stone fireplace with a stone slab mantel is on the back wall of the upper level. The ceiling is open to the huge ridgepole that is set in cement. Small-paned windows are on three sides of the building.

Edward and Ernest Feuz worked on the building, and it was finished at a cost of $2,500. The chalet was Swiss as was the hospitality: the Feuz family operated the tea house under the CPR license for fourteen years.

The CPR got a second building permit in 1927 and built three one-story cabins. There was overnight space for only a few guides and their clients, since the CPR did not want a full back-country "lodge" so close to one of its

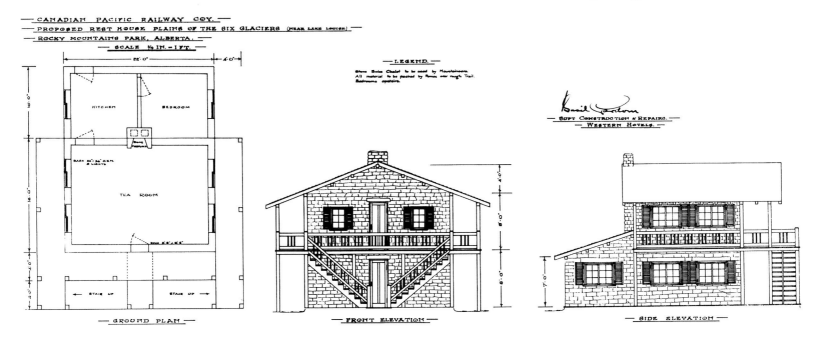

The Swiss inspired tea house was built as planned with the exception of the one-story kitchen off the back of the stone building.

major hotels. The company didn't get an official license to lease the small parcel of land until 1928. The railway signed a second twenty-one-year license of occupation in 1949. While the company divested itself of other backcountry properties during the 1950s, it wasn't until 1960 that Joy Kimball took over the CPR's tea house lease. She has been operating the tea house ever since.

The facility that Joy took over was much the same slice of Switzerland that Feuz and the CPR intended it to be. The roof has been reshingled and floors replaced, but the original stonework and masonry is still in place.

Overnight guests are no longer accommodated, but hikers and climbers still stop and fill the lovely balcony and inside tables and enjoy a pot of tea and lunch. The setting offers an almost surreal view of the mounts Lefroy and Victoria and their glaciers—very different from the classic postcard shots taken from Chateau Lake Louise.

The trail to Plain of Six Glaciers Tea House is one of the most popular in the region, and tourists flock from Lake Louise in droves during July and August. There is a slice of time from mid-September until the tea house closes in October, when the crowds dwindle along the trail. A spattering of alpine larch transforms into gold, and the remaining hikers can take a deep breath of crisp fall air and remind themselves that this tiny stone tea house is special.

Abbot Pass Hut and Plain of Six Gla-

*Waitresses in Swiss uniforms pose on the balcony of Plain of Six Glaciers Tea House, circa 1930.*

ciers Tea House are two architectural survivors of the genre from the Canadian Pacific Railway's great backcountry building spree. They are also stone solid reminders of the role the Swiss guides played in the development of the "Canadian Alps."

*Skoki Lodge is a National Historic Site and was originally built as a camp for local skiers.*

# SKOKI LODGE
## Banff National Park, Alberta

It is a 6.8-mile trek to Skoki Lodge. Whether taken by foot along the well trod summer trail or through winter snow on skis, each incline, each slope, each curve of the terrain is a new gift to the senses. Whether the warmth of summer has uncovered the alpine lakes or winter has smothered the tundra fields in snow, there is always the haunting cold grayness of the Slate Range: long stratified steps of rock held up like a shield against the sky.

That contrast of rock, snow, lakes, meadows and changing sky makes the trek so fascinating. While the trip can be challenging, Skoki Lodge guests get a jump start. A shuttle picks them up at Fish Creek parking lot and drops them at the trail head.

That was not the case in 1930 when Catharine and Peter Whyte, two newly married Banff artists, set out one autumn day to the site that was about to become Skoki Camp. That October, Catharine Whyte wrote her mother, Edith Robb, of their adventure:

"Clifford, Pete's older brother, is building a log cabin in Skoki Valley to stay in when out skiing, about twelve or more miles from Lake Louise station, up the Ptarmigan Valley and over two passes. It's quite high, the passes are above timber line and the skiing wonderful. Cyril Paris is building the cabin with Cliff, going into the ski business together. They were going out to see how the men building the cabin are get-

ting along and invited us. At 4:00 a.m. Sunday we went over to Cliff's for breakfast. Ike Mills…came with us. He has horses and is doing all the packing of supplies for Cliff. It was about 15° above, a chilly morning.

"We were pretty cold by the time we reached Lake Louise so we started ahead to keep warm…All the way up the steep hill they kept planning how it would be skiing down. The snow is deep up there, and the trees are small enough to be half-buried, so it wouldn't be bad to fall into, I'm hoping.

"We stopped for our lunch below the pass and made a fire and boiled some tea. Ike caught up to us…I could have ridden from then on but the boys were going over a different pass from the horses and I wanted to see if I could walk all the way. It was worth it, for we went down onto two turquoise colored lakes with a beautiful glacier above the upper lake…Then a mile or so across an open meadow to where the cabin is being built…The cabin is progressing well. The men were living in a teepee, the head man, Earl Spencer and Spud White, the axeman. They had a spruce tree they call their 'bear escape,' the branches cut, making it easy to climb up rapidly, for grizzlies don't climb trees.…Spud White showed me how to peel logs. We had another meal with them about 3:00, ham and tea, a loaf of bread, and jam. It was a long climb, though gradual, to the top of the pass, snow driving into our faces and pitch dark when we got to the top of the

**OPENED: SPRING 1931**
**BUILT BY: CLIFFORD WHITE, SR., AND CYRIL PARIS**

*The original cabin was a simple log design with SKOKI spelled out in branches on the roof.*

little hill. It was after 9:00 when we reached Banff. Cliff said it was at least twenty-six miles; quite a walk on trails that go up and down all the time."

—*October 8, 1930*

"Quite a walk on trails that go up and down all the time" still takes you to Skoki Valley cupped between the Wall of Jericho and Skoki Mountain. Most visitors arrive as the rich, late-afternoon sunlight casts long shadows through the Englemann spruce and alpine fir. Tightly set amidst the trees, Skoki Lodge is suddenly visible, its weathered logs in contrast to the greenery or glistening snow around it.

The first documented visit of the region by a non-native was in 1911, when James Foster Porter, of Winnetka, Illinois, organized a party and hired Banff outfitter Jimmy Simpson to explore the mountains east of Lake Louise. Porter, who had been exploring the Canadian Rockies for over a decade, and his companions suggested many of the names

in the region, including the "Skokie Valley." The spelling was revised to Skoki, an Indian word meaning "swamp." Porter seems to have been so taken with the name, that in 1940, the Chicago suburb of Niles City near his home of Winnetka, was renamed Skokie. The spectacular setting is about as far from the flat Chicago suburb as one can get.

The Canadian Pacific Railway and local outfitters had exploited such Rocky Mountain settings for summer pleasures. But the long months of winter held their own charms and tourist potential.

The Mount Norquay Ski Club, formed in 1926 and the forerunner to the Ski Club of the Canadian Rockies, built a ski hut and small ski jump, and cut runs north of Banff. The mountains certainly afforded more opportunities for ski development, and Cliff White and Cyril Paris set out to explore the Slate Range of Banff National Park in

search of the perfect location for a new ski camp. On the advice of some of the Swiss guides, they headed over Boulder and Deception passes to Skoki Valley. In the subalpine clearing that Catharine Whyte saw that autumn day, they built Skoki Lodge.

A license to operate a ski club and erect a cabin in the Skoki Valley was issued in August 1930 to the Mount Norquay Ski Club. In January 1930, Dominion Parks granted a five-year lease to the club. Besides Earl Spencer, who also built Catharine and Peter Whyte's Banff studio, and Spud White, others pitched in including Carl Knutsen and Austrian ski instructor Victor Kutschera.

They built a simple twenty-five-by-sixteen-foot peeled-spruce log cabin with a gable roof; the front roof extended over an open porch with small paned windows on each side of the door. The corners were saddle-notched in traditional rustic mountain design. Inside, a log near the front window still bears the words: "peeled by Mrs. Peter Whyte, October 6, 1930."

Branches spelling out SKOKI were fastened to the roof, and the lodge opened for skiers who relished the untouched, snow laden mountains, valleys and passes of the region.

The single story Halfway Hut was also built in 1931 as a stopping spot for guests traveling between Lake Louise railway station and the new lodge.

The Ski Club of the Canadian Rockies was formed that year and its share-holders, including Cliff and Cyril, took over the financing of lodge construction and operation. By the end of 1931, all was not financially well with The Ski Club's Skoki operation.

"We have actually gone into the ski business," Catharine Whyte again wrote her mother. "It seems to us a wonderful idea. If we hadn't done it there wasn't anyone else who could, and it meant no camp this year and a black eye to skiing round here."

The "wonderful" idea included the Whytes' taking over the debt incurred by construction of cabins and a kitchen extension at Skoki that summer, according to Catharine's letters. The Skoki Ski Camp bail-out may well have been the first of the Whytes' philanthropic endeavors.

The lovely blue blood from a prominent New England family had met the dashing Peter at Boston's Museum of Fine Arts School in 1925. They courted and he introduced her to the mountains and a life she enthusiastically embraced. They married in 1930, and while they were world travelers, for over thirty years the two painted, sketched, skied, hiked and became an integral part of the Canadian Rocky Mountains. Pete died in 1966 at the age of 61, and Catharine lived until 1979. The Whyte Museum of the Canadian Rockies in Banff began as a foundation endowed by the Whytes and evolved into the gallery, museum and archives

*Peter Whyte, who with his wife Catharine backed and managed the lodge, snapped this picture of friends and clients during the 1932 ski season, right. Supplies were hauled in by sled dogs or on the backs of skiers.*

*When it was time to expand in 1936, the lodge got a new addition and the second floor was redesigned for guest rooms, below.*

that it is today. The Whytes' house and studio is part of the park of heritage buildings.

At Skoki, the Whytes did more than carry the debt. The young couple managed the operation, including the log Halfway Hut, during the 1931-32 and 1932-33 seasons. It took planning and just plain hard work. By the spring of 1932, Pete estimated that their crew of eight men and two dog teams had brought in over 3200 pounds of provisions, bedding and stoves. "We packed in four stoves! 14 miles! Over two mountain passes!" he wrote to his mother-in-law.

The Whytes were popular managers and business grew steadily. In the summer of 1932, two additional cabins were built, now named Raven and Wolverine. Each followed the Standard Plan for backcountry cabins drawn in 1918 by James Childe for Dominion Parks. The Skoki camp cabins are somewhat larger at sixteen by twenty feet, with steeply pitched gable roofs and deep overhangs to cover the wooden porches. Large spruce beams support the shingled roofs and the buildings are constructed of locally harvested logs with saddle-notched corners. Two paned-windows flank the front door and two side-windows let in additional light. Inside, wood-burning stoves once heated the simply furnished cabins.

But in the spring of 1933 tragedy struck. A young client, Raymond "Kit" Paley, out skiing on his own, was caught in an avalanche on Fossil Mountain. Giving up the search because of darkness and cold, Pete and another skier found his body the following day. The accident deeply affected Catharine and Pete. They closed up camp for the season at the end of May and returned to Banff. "…[T]he let-down was terrific after we came in from the camp, and we couldn't seem to get the thing out of our minds," Catharine wrote her mother.

Jim Boyce had cooked for the Whytes that winter and when Skoki reopened for the summer season, Boyce took over as manager. Boyce continued to operate Skoki through the 1930s.

During that time, skiing was becoming increasingly popular, and in 1935-36 Boyce expanded the camp, still under the aegis of the Ski Club of the Canadian Rockies, with major shareholders being Sir Norman Watson and Catharine Whyte. Among Sir Norman Watson's many plans was to construct a network of cabins that would have linked Skoki, Red Deer Valley and the Pipestone. The outbreak of World War II ended that particular dream.

Boyce hired Earl Spencer as the Skoki Lodge job foreman. The plan was to add a first floor extension nearly doubling the size of the main floor. The addition would have a stone fireplace; the old one with sand mortar had proven problematic. The original cabin had bunks, but Spencer planned to add guest rooms upstairs. Three dormers were added to the front of the lodge and

*Peeled log walls, a huge stone fireplace and plenty of spots to curl up and read make the living room at Skoki the heartbeat of the lodge.*

a large double dormer to the back.

By October the lower floor was nearly finished, but Spencer needed an experienced axeman to complete the job. His friend George Harrison found his man, and in the fall of 1936, Ken Jones showed up at Skoki. Jones was not only a fine axeman, but the first Canadian-born mountain guide in the Rockies.

Jones' first task was to find a sixty-foot ridgepole to run the length of the lodge plus the addition. Ken found the tree about eight miles away, near Red Deer River. It took five men and four horses to get the log to the site: "And it was pretty tough going," recalled Ken, who was at the lodge in the summer of 1998 for his annual working visit.

The ridgepole and twenty-seven rafters were used green to frame the roof. The ridgepole was one tree, but the side purlins were spliced at an angle to link the original lodge to the addition. The log corners are butt joined with a round notched interior log to cover the connection. "Valley" and "Jack" rafters were used around the dormers and all of the intricate log work is still visible in the guest rooms. The roof was covered in shiplap lumber with taper tip shakes finishing the job. Fir was shipped from the West Coast for the floors.

The walls are not paper thin, rather a single layer of shiplap lumber held by lateral studding divides the rooms. As with all backcountry lodges, privacy is an illusion. The Skoki, Merlin and Molar guest

rooms face the front with the considerably smaller Fossil, Deception and Silver Tip guest rooms, and storage, tucked along the back. On the landing is a communal sink (no running water) and reading space. The bathrooms are his and her outhouses behind the wood shed.

*Tiny Honeymoon Cabin is tucked in the trees, a perfect hideaway for summer guests.*

Boyce and Jones built the quarter-turn stairway with landing in the addition's corner while waiting for the park warden to show up and kill a wolverine. "We put in a log post and beam frame, then we both took a whack at it," said Jones, who at that point was more willing to take a "whack" at the staircase

than another try at trapping the vicious wolverine that had already ruined the cabin now bearing its name.

The new living room was accessed by a large entry cut between the two rooms. While the walls are peeled spruce logs caulked with ship building grade oakum, unpeeled larch was used to frame the windows and doors. A stone fireplace with an arched hearth and roughhewn wood mantle now has a more efficient fireplace insert.

Most of the furniture and built-in window seats that double as bunks were made on site and are still favorite spots where guests curl up to read or nap. The buffet table still used today was made from off-cuts from the stair treads, and the stools are log ends left over from construction. The lodge even had thirty-two-volt electricity from a single cylinder diesel-motor generator.

But the main lodge wasn't the only expansion. In 1936, a twenty-six by-twenty-foot log bathhouse was built with two small gables extending over the doors: one for ladies and the other for gentlemen. Water was pumped from the creek into a tank for showers—a luxury not afforded modern-day guests. A side entrance accessed a room for ski maintenance and storage.

Simple sixteen-by-twenty-foot Honeymoon and Creek (now Riverside) cabins, constructed in much the same manner as the Wolverine and Raven cabins, were also built that year.

By Christmas of 1936, the lodge ex-

*The logwork, including Jack and Valley rafters, is clearly visible in a guest room built as part of the 1936 addition. The indoor bathroom facilities are a bowl and pitcher, right. "Backcountry" means no indoor plumbing.*

pansion was complete, and business began to boom. Guests arrived at the Lake Louise train station then skied in to Skoki. What was once a secret retreat for locals was getting international attention. Guides met the guests at the station, loaded up supplies and escorted the skiers to the lodge with stopovers at Halfway Hut.

"In 1936 Skoki was the most ritzy place north of Sun Valley," exclaimed Jones. Now 87 years old, he still spends part of each summer working at Skoki and Mount Assiniboine lodges.

Other Canadian Rockies characters managed Skoki over the years, including Lizzie Rummel, who was here from 1942 to 1949 then moved on to Assiniboine and Sunburst camps in Mount Assiniboine Provincial Park. Ray Lagace, Bert and June Mickle, and Paul Peyto all took a hand at operating the lodge and cabins. Until the 1970s, summer clients came by horse, most outfitted by what became Timberline Tours. Though Timberline still takes guests by horseback into Skoki, most come on foot today. The Ski Club's shareholders held the lease until 1972, when Charlie Locke and Village Lake Louise, Ltd.

took over ownership.

From 1979 to 1988 a variety of individuals operated the lodge in both summer and winter. In 1988, Blake O'Brian took over management with ownership continuing under Locke's Resorts of the Canadian Rockies.

"Skoki Ski Lodge" and the five surrounding buildings were designated a National Historic Site in 1992, one of the few such designations in the Canadian Rocky Mountain parks.

Over six decades of varied management changes seem so subtle as to be unnoticed by guests. The electricity was removed in the early 1960s, and pine cones, not light bulbs, are screwed into the old light sockets. Kerosene lamps now light the rooms offering just enough light for the evening's ambiance. With the exception of one cold water tap in the kitchen, there is still no indoor plumbing, and the bathhouse was converted to a staff cabin.

Guests' morning routine involves fetching water from warming kettles on the wood-burning stove and carrying it to their rooms or cabins. The first person who wakes up is the alarm clock for others—the entire second floor creaks like the piece of history that it is. There is a wood-burning sauna that is a wonderful stop after a quick "bath" in the frigid creek.

The original doors were replaced in 1996 with wooden doors with thermal-pane glass windows. Much of the original furniture is gone, but every detail has the historic integrity of the site in mind. The dining tables and chairs, where some of the finest food in the Canadian Rockies is served, are all hand-made. And Blake enjoys hand-finishing bent wood into coat hooks, door pulls or any other use that he fancies. A gallery of historic black and white photographs, hung along with skiing memorabilia, adds to the historic charm. Copies of Peter and Catharine Whyte's landscape paintings hang in the guest rooms. The big kitchen, where something is always under preparation, was "modernized" with a propane stove.

It is a summer afternoon, and chef Kim Purdy tucks plump cloves of garlic into the huge beef tenderloin being readied for dinner. Out the kitchen door and behind the lodge, acting manager Walter Odenthal takes a break under an oversized umbrella festooned with netting—his latest defense against mosquitoes. Ken Jones puts away his axe to play fetch with Colors, the dog of unknown heritage. Ken throws the ball which beans the dog. Colors screeches to a halt, Ken holds his hand to his whiskered chin, the umbrella tips back, the kitchen door opens and everyone bursts into laughter.

The scene is the kind of interlude that brings to life this National Historic Site.

*The dining room is in the original portion of the lodge; the large opening was cut for access to the addition.*

*The CPR requested permission to build Mount Assiniboine Lodge as a link in the railway's camp tour.*

By air is not how ski pioneers Erling Strom and Marquis delgi Albizzi arrived at the edge of Magog Lake in 1928. Certainly not how American businessman and mountaineer Robert L. Barrett and his Banff guide, Tom Wilson, made the first recorded trip by white men to the base of Mount Assiniboine in 1893. Father Pierre-Jean de Smet, who laid eyes on it in 1845, may have had even more of a religious epiphany if he had seen what he called "this great architectural cliff" from our vantage point.

But we are not cross-country skiing over Assiniboine Pass or hiking the seventeen miles along Bryant Creek. With the excuse of heavy photo equipment and limited time, we board a six-passenger Astar helicopter at Mount Shark Heli-port for a fifteen minute flight to Mount Assiniboine Lodge.

After we are boarded and briefed by our pilot, the din becomes a roar and we are up. A full Panavision view fills the glass front of the cockpit. Watridge Lake is a fleeting blue dot below us, then we skirt the southwestern arm of Spray Lakes Reservoir, and are immediately flanked by the unforgiving faces of

Mount Turner on the left and Cone Mountain on the right as we head up Bryant Creek Valley and over Assiniboine Pass. Bryant Creek twists a ribbon through the lush valley floor that looks as well groomed as a golf course fairway. Sliver-thin waterfalls cut another stratified reach of rock as we bank to

the left, then below us are the chartreuse watercolor-swirl of an unnamed pond and the deep-blue leggy Marvel Lake. Behind Marvel, Lake Gloria glistens teal beneath an amphitheater of glacial ice. As we approach Lake Magog, the red roofs of the lodge complex appear like buildings on a wilderness version of a Monopoly game board. Mount Assiniboine looms on the west-

ern shore, a dominant presence rising like one huge block of rock precisely chiseled into a towering spire. We drop to a heli-pad and are quickly hustled away.

Or we could have walked.

Early mountaineers, surveyors and adventurers gazed at 11,780-foot Mount Assiniboine and saw their "Matterhorn." The stony likeness of the peak that cuts the Continental Divide and the infamous Swiss mountain warrant comparison. But to the first surveyors, the seemingly sheer cliffs of Assiniboine seemed unattainable, which only prompted its ascent. In 1899, Walter Wilcox, who had surveyed the Assiniboine region, and two other climbers made an unsuccessful attempt of the summit. Wilcox returned in 1901, this time with Swiss guides, but was again thwarted by treacherous conditions.

In 1901, Edward Whymper, at the invitation of the Canadian Pacific Railway, was brought with much fanfare to the "Canadian Alps." His hosts hoped that the man who conquered the Matterhorn would make the first ascent of Mount Assiniboine—as the railway

*Marquis delgi Albizzi and Erling Strom saw Assiniboine as the perfect ski camp, above. The lodge continues to cater to those looking for a winter ski getaway, below.*

liked to say, the highest peak south of the CPR line. The potential for advertising and marketing was too tantalizing for words. But Whymper, then sixty-one, turned his back on the thirty-square-mile beast of a mountain and focused on tamer quests.

It would be James Outram, a young English vicar who found challenge and solace in the Canadian Rockies, who would be the first man to scale the peak. With two Swiss guides, Christian Häsler and Christian Bohren, and Banff outfitter and guide Bill Peyto, Outram reached the peak of Mount Assiniboine on September 3, 1901.

Not until 1922 were 12,850 acres set aside as Mount Assiniboine Provincial Park. A.O. Wheeler, who had mapped the Assiniboine area and was the first president of the Alpine Club of Canada, promoted protecting the region by making it a park. Wheeler acquired freehold right to forty-four acres of land around Lake Magog in 1920, and established a camp as part of rigorous seventy-five-mile circuit Walking Tours.

Having secured the site, he sold the acreage to the ACC, and the club leased the land back to him in 1924. The following summer, Wheeler built a group of log cabins on the edge of a small meadow at the lake's north end. Wonder Lodge anchored the little log community now called Naiset Cabins, and there most of the guests stayed.

The CPR was building pack trails of its own, and the company's Bungalow Camps in the Canadian Rockies tours were in full swing. On November 15, 1926, Basil Gardom wrote the British Columbia minister of lands informing him that the CPR was considering developing a bungalow camp at Mount Assiniboine. It would be part of the route mapped out by Gardom to parks brass the following year that would begin at the "head of Brewster Creek, on to our Mount Assiniboine Camp, to Sunshine valley, to Shadow Lake, to Storm Mountain Camp [now Castle Mountain Camp], to Moraine Lake, to Wapta, to Lake O'Hara, then via Ottertail Cabin to Emerald Lake Chalet, via Natural Bridge, then via Summit Lake

Rest House to Twin Falls Chalet to Yoho Camp, returning to Wapta Camp" then to the train.

The railway was interested in fifty acres adjoining the ACC plot, along Lake Magog. The lease was approved and issued to the CPR in February 1927. By January 1928, the CPR's plans had become so grandiose that Gardom, on behalf of the company, applied to the Provincial government's minister of lands for a twenty-one-year lease covering the entire twenty-square-mile Mount Assiniboine Park Reserve, including the ACC property: "I request the privilege of having this area known as the 'Canadian Pacific Park at Mount Assiniboine'." The request was denied.

Meanwhile, Wheeler's Walking Tours had exhausted the hearty hikers, and he sublet the Assiniboine property to Marquis delgi Albizzi, not for walking, but for skiing. Albizzi, a suave and well-known European count and skier had seen the area in the summer, and envisioned a wonderland covered in white. Albizzi was winter sports director of Lake Placid, New York, and he suggested to Lake Placid ski instructor and friend, Erling Strom, that they organize ski trips into Assiniboine.

On March 5, 1928, Strom, Albizzi and four clients left Banff for their great ski adventure. Although there was no snow to be seen in town the intrepid group of six struck out as Banffites shook their heads in disbelief. The trip was long and eventful, but the pay-off

*The moon over Mount Assiniboine is reflected in a small pond.*

*Erling Strom sits on the original log and elk-hide couch that is still used today, circa 1955. Strom painted the door and the Viking dragon above it, right.*

*The room became the main dining room when the addition was completed, above right.*

*Barb Renner, above, produces amazing meals and loaf upon loaf of bread from the kitchen.*

came in seventeen days of sunshine and skiing that dreams are made of—and plenty of snow. Strom's mind was quickly made up: if he could swing it, Assiniboine was going to be the place where he would spend most of his life.

Albizzi thought the area was spectacular, but the cabins unsuitable for the clientele he envisioned attracting. Upon their return, Albizzi contacted the CPR, and according to Strom, "No sooner were we back to civilization than he...told them that if they would build us a camp at Assiniboine the two of us could keep it going summer and winter because of our connection with Lake Placid Club."

The railway already had the land lease in hand, so that summer a railway crew was dispatched to build the camp. Unfortunately, unbeknownst to those involved, the Park Act of 1911, which had facilitated the later establishment of Mount Assiniboine Park by Order-in-Council, made authorization of that lease void. It took until five years after the new lodge and cabins opened for the CPR and the government to sign a twenty-one-year lease that in essence took the fifty-acre plot out of the park.

Albizzi operated the lodge for its first summer season in 1929 while Strom

was in Norway. The count became disillusioned with the difficulties of operating a backcountry camp, and the CPR rented the camp to Mrs. Bill (Missy) Brewster; Strom took over winter operation. (The winter season was from two

*The front porch of the original portion of the lodge is still a favorite congregating spot for summer guests. The porch tables were the first dining tables.*

to four weeks in March and April.)

Strom, who still saw his life to be lived at Assiniboine, made an offer to buy the camp and the lease from the CPR in late 1935. The railway sought approval from the province's lands de-

partment for assignment of the lease to Storm or the reissuing of a new lease. In April 1936, Strom purchased the camp and its furnishings from the railway, and sublet the fifty-acre lot from the railway, signing a twenty-one-year sublease that became official the following November.

The complex consisted of a main cabin for cooking, dining and relaxing, six guest cabins and a sauna. A two-story addition began in 1958.

The original lodge is a twenty-four-by-eighteen-foot room with adjoining sixteen-by-sixteen-foot kitchen of peeled-log, saddle-notched construction. The pitched roof stretches over a ridgepole and six purlins extend forming a generous front porch. Four upright timbers and a cross beam support the roof with a center collar adding to the framing. The cabin was situated according to Strom's specifications so that the heavy winter snow that could easily bury the building left the front entrance accessible.

But winter still got the best of the building, and in 1935, half of the roof blew away. "There were white caps on my tea cup right before the roof blew off," explained Ken Jones, decades later. When asked what he did, "Jonesy," a regular Assiniboine mountain guide and

*The stucco-covered chimney of the main lounge is decorated with rosmaling. Original French Canadian-style log and elk-hide furniture has been supplemented with pieces handmade by Sepp Renner.*

former park ranger replied, "I put my hand over the cup."

A belfry tower and dinner bell were added in the early 1960s giving perhaps a false sense of anchor for the roof. Metal roofs were added to the buildings in 1984.

Inside, Strom painted an orange and green Viking dragon on the interior wall over the front door and windows, the beginning of decorative painting that

has been added to the lodge over the years. Within the belly of the dragon are legendary names—Erling Strom, Sam Evans, Marquis delgi Albizzi, Elizabeth Fruin Von Rummel, Nicolas Morant—still preserved as written. Above the dragon are Russell Bennett's wooden skis used when he skied into Assiniboine in 1929. His son, Winslow Bennett, gave the skis to the lodge, and like the families of many early guests, the

Bennetts still vacation at Assiniboine.

Since the lodge was meant for winter use, collar beams and scissors braces support the coffered wood ceiling, thus adding an insulating layer to the roof. The room once had a loft primarily used for storage. Old timers say that's where Erling kept the rum for his famous Cougar Milk, a concoction made with hot water, sweetened condensed milk, nutmeg and ample rum. After a day of skiing, a mug of Cougar Milk in hand, guests lounged on the log-pole and elk-hide couches and chairs built by the wranglers, and propped their feet on split log benches.

The log walls were originally chinked with oakum and wooden slates. In 1984, the logs were cleaned, bleached and varnished and rechinked with cement. Three years later, all of the windows were replaced with thermal glass, and the original wooden door with rosemaling on the inside was replaced by a windowed door. A new wood coffered ceiling, built in the same fashion as the original, was added in 1983 to hold a layer of insulation.

Propane brass lights hang from the ceiling, and the cabin now serves as the dining room and kitchen where wondrous meals, and loaf upon loaf of bread and pastries are prepared. Platters and bowls of food are served family style to hikers and skiers who sit on chairs handmade by old-time wrangler Charlie Hunter, at newer handmade birch tables. No one leaves hungry or disappointed. The kitchen was remodeled and updated in 1985, and it now has refrigeration, light and hot running water.

The original dining room tables are now on the front porch and the rustic log-slab chairs serve as outdoor furniture at the cabins.

Six simple peeled-log cabins that follow the much adapted parks' 1918 Standard Plan were built on stone foundations and are dotted along the footpath. The saddle-notched corners are stepped on the front to support the small overhang that shelters each porch stoop. As with the main lodge, the apex of the pitched roof is sectioned off by collar beams and a coffered ceiling. In 1984, the cabin roofs were insulated and pine ceilings installed following the same design as the original ceiling.

Rooms were simply furnished, and the first guests slept on "banana beds" —two poles with a canvas sling "mattress." Guest Betty Hermann describes her cabin in 1938: "My diary description of the cabins is as follows: Hang clothes on beam, beds sag in middle. Writing this by candlelight."

Today, handmade wooden bedframes (with real mattresses), down comforters, a washstand with piped in cold water, a propane heat stove, tables and chairs and views—always views—offer coziness after a day of hiking or skiing. You can write by propane light.

The Great Depression and downhill skiing impacted the ski touring plans, and the lodge closed for winter in the

late 1930s. But summer travelers still flocked through the valley and over passes to Lake Magog's pristine shores. The Alpine Club of Canada had its Climbing Camp at Assiniboine in 1920 and at Assiniboine Park in 1935, and the Trail Riders of the Canadian Rockies, whose first trip to Assiniboine was in 1927, returned regularly as did the Sky Line Trail Hikers of the Canadian Rockies, a sister group.

Trail riding became the favored form of travel to Assiniboine during the summer, and Strom along with the Brewsters and other outfitters brought hun-

*The saddle-notched peeled log cabins offer a bit of privacy in the wilderness.*

*Inside each cabin the coffered wood ceilings, handmade bedframes, down comforters and propane heaters create simple comfortable retreats.*

dreds of trail riders to the area.

When skiing resumed after World War II, Erling leased the lodge to Larry Boyd from 1945 to 1950. It was decided that more skiers would come to the remote reaches of Assiniboine if they could fly in. Al Gaetz, manager of the Inter-Mountain Airlines, flew the first guests to the lodge, and in 1952, he requested parks approval of a small airstrip, 1,200 to 1,500 feet long and twenty-five feet wide. Skiing in may have been exhausting, but the flight and landing could be terrifying. Many guests flew in then opted to ski out.

Erling Strom continued to operate the lodge with the help of a rotating group of staff and managers who inevitably became friends and part of the Assiniboine family. Lizzie Rummel, who later opened Sunburst Cabins at Sunburst Lake; Ken Jones, who became the first ranger of Assiniboine Provincial Park in 1967 and helped build Skoki and Num-Ti-Jah lodges; Al Johnston, Erling's partner for a time, were a few. Erling and his wife Sigrid also owned and managed a lodge in Stowe, Vermont; they had one daughter, Siri, who eventually managed the Assiniboine Lodge. It was not unusual for guests to fill in when a cook was needed or for other jobs around camp.

In 1950, Erling began a Christmas newsletter for clients and staff, *The Assiniboine Wrangler*, a combination of lodge updates, park policies, ski, riding and hiking tips and charming, folksy gossip. Through it Strom rallied his loyal troops when parks policy infringed on his operation.

In 1955, Erling attempted to purchase the fifty-acre lot that the CPR had excluded from the park in 1933. Instead, the lot was reincorporated into Mount Assiniboine Provincial Park, and in 1957, Erling and Al Johnston were issued a twenty-one-year Park-Use Permit for six acres. In 1965, Erling received $15,000 compensation for the original buildings that became Crown property when the fifty-acre lot was added to the Provincial Park; he continued to operate the lodge.

Over the years, Erling had used the Naiset Cabins for storage and overflow guests. In 1950 he built a small Pack Shack where wranglers, saddles and tack were "packed." Today, lodge managers Barb and Sepp Renner, still call it "The Mighty-fine Gentleman's Club." By the late 1950s, things were going well enough that Erling decided to expand the lodge.

Strom appreciated the art of log work, and hired Dave Leslie for the job. Leslie spent four summers creating the peeled log, two-story addition, and Provincial Park records indicate that Strom was paid, over time, $22,886.93 for the new lodge construction.

"Log building is rapidly becoming a lost art. Few people have seen it done. Fewer can do it. Our guests were fascinated all summer by watching Dave Leslie adding log by log to what will be a second half of our main building," Strom wrote in the December 1958 *Wrangler*. "Dave is one of the last living good builders, at least on this side of the ocean, with the necessary know-how, skill, patience, and pride in his work to do a perfect job." And perfect it is.

Strom had been collecting suitable logs over the years, but other supplies had to be packed in. Strom estimated that he and Al Johnston loaded 130 head of horses with lumber and materials for thirty-four round trips from Banff to Assiniboine. Each horse was packed with two bundles of ten to fourteen boards, each cut to six- or seven-

foot lengths. The twenty-five-mile trips took two days, and everything was unloaded then repacked at Halfway Hut.

The first floor of the addition is twenty-nine by eighteen feet with saddle-notched corners; an interior log wall di-

*Decorative rosmaling, as on the doorway to the main lounge, has been added over the years.*

vides the lounge from the entry, bathroom and stairway. The Norwegian design features a wind scour and overhangs to protect it from blowing snow. The top log ends are stepped to support the second story that overhangs the main floor. Each log is so tightly linked

to the next that Erling declared you couldn't slip a knife between them.

Leslie worked alone hoisting the huge logs. He placed two logs at angles from the ground to the wall, then slid the construction log in place using ropes fastened on each end. "By going back and forth pulling a little on one rope and then the other he can move the log up slowly. It is then fitted to the one below in such a way that the chinking between can not be seen from either side of the wall, Scandinavian style. If the roof is maintained, Dave's building will be there 500 years from now," wrote Strom in the *Wrangler*.

Inside, a corner fireplace sits on a stone hearth; the stucco-covered cement chimney painted with rosemaling is the centerpiece of the room. Hand-hewn cross beams and peeled logs support the second floor, and angled planks finish the ceiling. The original wooden floors reflect the tracks of time. French Canadian-style log and elk-hide furniture from the original cabin was moved in, and Sepp Renner made additional pieces. Historic memorabilia and photographs, rosemaling, books and even Whymper's ice ax add to the room's charm. Small-paned windows fill three walls, and hazy light drifts through space.

A small bathroom with running hot water, shower and a flush toilet (almost unheard of in backcountry lodges) is off the entry. A root cellar is under the entry floorboards. Almost useless after years of water damage, it was renovated

*Walking, cross country skiing and trail riding were the original modes of transportation into Mount Assiniboine. Today, guests and goods can be flown in on a limited basis.*

and is used for storage and part of the battery-charged generator system that provides 12-volt light to the main lodge and kitchen. A steep, open log-framed stairway takes guests to the second floor. Plank walls, angled ceiling and small paned windows give the rooms individual charm. Wildfowers are painted on each door: Erling's Room has alpine forget-me-nots.

Apparently a guest from New York, who signed his or her work "Frost," did much of the decorative painting on the doors between 1960 and 1963. The upright carved front-porch timbers also got a touch of color during this time when new doors were hung and painted in the breezeway connecting the two buildings.

As Erling's lease expiration date approached, the man who had become synonymous with Assiniboine Lodge thought of retirement. He started looking for a suitable party to be issued a long-term Park-Use Permit and take over the lodge. But the government had other ideas.

In 1970, the *Wrangler* was not full of its usual upbeat chatter: "Please consider this a personal letter to all Assiniboine friends, and read it carefully. The Lodge, such as we know it, is doomed unless I get a great deal of help to do something about it. What I have tried to create, and I dare say succeeded in creating, will be gone forever, unless we can get the present plans for Assiniboine Park changed. The Park Planner have decided to withdraw my permit altogether when my time is up, and turn the Lodge into a Government Hostel…a regular Hippie Haven is more than I can stand. Assiniboine Lodge is too good for that."

Park Director R.H. Ahrens finally ruled in favor of continuing Assiniboine as a privately operated lodge on public land. Erling retired and said good-bye to his beloved Assiniboine Lodge in 1978. Other members of the Strom family operated Assiniboine until 1983, when Barb and Sepp Renner took over as concessionaires. During most of that time, Assiniboine Lodge Ltd. and B.C. Parks have restored and rehabilitated the buildings. While the work has by backcountry terms been extensive, the lodge, cabins and grounds seem virtually the same as when Erling held court in the evening before guests.

The Pack Shack is now staff housing, and the dilapidated barn was renovated, expanded and converted to the Renners' home and office. Work is continuous and oftentimes not glamorous. Waterlines, dams, outhouses, floors and foundations fill a long list of work projects. In 1995, much to guests' delight, a sauna/showerhouse was built on the site of the old sauna.

But the most obvious change at Assiniboine was the switch from pack horses to helicopters for transporting supplies and guests. The old corral, once a maze of mud, was dismantled and landscape restored, and in 1984, helicopters began shuttling guests and supplies to the lodge. Three years later the Provincial Park increased flight access to three flight days a week, and greater lodge visitorship came with it. Over the next decade a see-saw struggle ensued between park visitors and park regulators concerning acceptable levels of helicopter access. The future of the lodge itself was also at stake. The lodge remains today a living testament to those who love Canadian history—both cultural and natural.

Since the days of A.O. Wheeler's Walking Tours, hiking is and has been more than the means of arrival. Guests set out each day on treks guided by Sepp, Barb or qualified staff. Mountaineering is popular and hikers appear at the lodge for tea. Just getting to Assiniboine Lodge adds to its appeal.

Once here, it is difficult to leave.

It is nearly impossible to pull myself from under the down-filled comforter, but the moon is peeking over Mount Assiniboine, and there is a new light on Lake Magog. Only a few hours later, in skies that never remain the same, the first sunlight spreads a pale pink alpenglow softening the hulk of glacier ice cradled between Mount Assiniboine and Mount Strom. Fog hovers on the

*Early mountaineers, surveyors and adventurers gazed at the 11,780-foot peak of Mount Assiniboine and saw their Matterhorn.*

glassy surface of the lake, and in a blink, it is gone, replaced by gray clouds. The heavy night of rain has left everything moist and pristine.

I crawl back into bed until I hear a cheerful, Swiss laced, "Good morning!" Sepp parks a pail of steaming water on the porch stoop. Good morning, indeed!

I pour the water into the brightly painted metal basin and find total luxury as I stand at a window of the Strom

cabin and watch the morning scene. I contemplate our departure. The clouds are heavy and the mist is now rain. The helicopters flights are rarely canceled on account of weather. I close my eyes and recall the exhilarating flight in. The sweep through the Bryant Creek Valley and over Assiniboine Pass, the lakes and creeks and towering cliffs of sheer, unforgiving rock.

Or we could always walk.

*The original log CPR cabin stands between two new cabins flanking the edge of the forest.*

In May 1929, the *Trail Riders of the Canadian Rockies Bulletin* outlined the summer's trips including a twenty-six-mile, four-day ride from Banff to Castle Mountain Bungalow Camp. The group would camp at Shadow Lake, which "…has excellent camping ground, and the Canadian Pacific is building a rest house, as the proposed trail ride will undoubtedly attract many riders after the Trail Riders have gone over it."

The route would form half the group's long-wished-for High Line Trail from Banff to Lake Louise. After the stop at Castle Mountain, the Trail Riders 1929 backcountry ride would continue four days later, giving participants plenty of time to stay at the company's bungalow camp or return to Lake Louise or Banff where they could frequent the Canadian Pacific Railway's pricey hotels, then pick up the other half of the trip, and return home using the rail line.

Obviously, the CPR had a vested interest in the trail.

Anyone with a hankering to see the Canadian Rockies could do so with the help of the CPR, Brewster Transport Company or one of the family members' offshoot operations. The network of lodging and travel options was almost incestuous, and each link meant more choices for the growing number of post World War I travelers. Groups like the CPR-inspired Trail Riders and its sister group the Sky Line Trail Hikers of the Canadian Rockies offered instant

camaraderie to those seeking backcountry adventure.

In October 1927, Basil Gardom applied for two five-acre sites at Shadow Lake and Sunshine Valley, "to form connecting links in our Company's chain of camps in this region." A few days earlier Gertrude Crosby (wife of Lou Crosby of the Brewster Transport Company and manager of Deer Lodge at Lake Louise) applied for a five-acre plot of land at the lake's northeast end for a "high class" tea room and cabins.

Mrs. Crosby's tea room and cabins were never built, but the CPR's rest house, located one-half mile from the lake on the brim of a subalpine meadow, was completed for the 1930 season. The railway had planned to build three stop-over cabins along the new route: one at Brewster Creek, another in Sunshine Valley and the third at a previously used campsite near Shadow Lake. Brewster and Sunshine sites offered few problems, but the two Shadow Lake applications slowed the parks' permit decision. On October 31, 1928, the CPR received a building permit to construct a stop-over cabin with a minimum value of $1,500 on a site selected by the parks' Chief Warden, the legendary Bill Peyto. The following April, a request to cut forty green logs was approved, and Peyto was instructed to mark the trees before they were cut.

The railway submitted the *C.P.R. Stop-Over Log Cabin* plan for all three

---

**OPENED: 1930 (ORIGINAL REST HOUSE)**
**1991-1997 (ADDITIONAL CABINS)**
**BUILT BY: CANADIAN PACIFIC RAILWAY (ORIGINAL REST HOUSE)**
**BUD BREWSTER (ADDITIONAL CABINS)**

buildings, calling for flat stone foundation with hewn pole floor joists mortised into the bottom logs and built of even-sized peeled logs with tight notched corners. The Shadow Lake cabin adhered to the CPR's plan for a twenty-by-twenty-four-foot building partitioned into three rooms, but the log and detail work surpasses other buildings of this genre.

The Shadow Lake cabin was built of green timber instead of the preferable seasoned wood, and the logs were "kerfed" or slit to account for shrinkage as the trees dried. The logs are stacked in reverse-taper fashion, the corners are meticulously saddle-notched, and the deep, cantilevered, front-verandah overhang is further supported by perfectly stepped logs protruding from each side of the cabin. There is a centered front door flanked by two large paned windows framed by split peeled logs; two smaller windows are on the back wall. The gable roof, supported by a ridge-pole and eight purlins, was covered in cedar wood shingles.

When finished, the cabin was not a revenue-generating venture. Rather, it was available to the public as basic shelter along the popular trail. The Sky Line Trail Hikers May 1935 *Bulletin* announced that summer's trip would begin at Sunshine Valley and end at Castle Mountain with stops at Egypt Lake and Shadow Lake, where the CPR cabin "has 12 bunks for the first twelve ladies who make reservations." The accommodations were simple but free—compliments of the CPR.

By the time Shadow Lake Cabin was completed in March 1930, Basil Gardom had retired, and J.A. Angus had become superintendent of construction and maintenance for the railway's western hotels. Shadow Lake would be the CPR's swan song in the backcountry.

Brewster Creek cabin, Shadow Lake Rest House and Sunshine Lodge were three log and shingle links in the CPR's grand plan—a plan that by the time Shadow Lake was finally finished was shifting.

The Depression and changing travel tastes forced the CPR to reanalyze its focus. The company concentrated on its major hotels—Banff and Chateau Lake Louise—along with its deluxe bungalow camps, and began divesting itself of smaller operations. In 1934, Jim Brewster of Brewster Transport Company got permission from the CPR to use Sunshine cabin for another purpose—skiing. Brewster officially took Sunshine

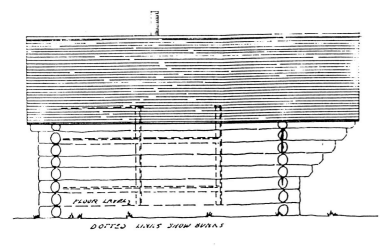

SIDE ELEVATION

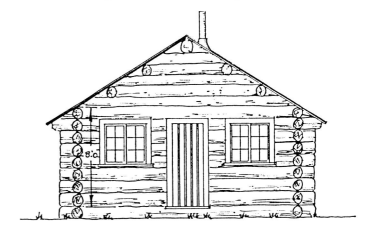

FRONT ELEVATION.

*The CPR submitted plans for three Stop-Over Log Cabins to form connecting links in the company's chain of camps in the region. Shadow Lake plans were dated Dec. 31, 1927 and signed by Basil Gardom.*

off the CPR's hands in 1936 when he purchased the railway's license of occupation on the cabin and land. He immediately began constructing a twenty-four-by-forty, two-story addition to the original CPR cabin.

Erling Strom took over the CPR's lease at Brewster Cabin and Mount Assiniboine Lodge in 1936. In 1938, the CPR informed R.A. Gibson, parks branch director in Ottawa, that the railway was also disposing of the Shadow Lake Rest House to Mr. James Brewster, "it being the latter's intention to enlarge, improve and furnish it for the use of riding and fishing parties in the summer, and skiing parties in the winter, operating it in conjunction with his Sunshine Valley Camp."

In October of that year, Jim Brewster and Brewster Transport Co. were granted the lease on Shadow Lake Rest House. Parks Superintendent P.J. Jennings, well aware of Brewster's quick expansion at Sunshine, reminded Mr. Brewster that "no development whatsoever must be undertaken on the site" without approval. Expansion was not forthcoming, and the cabin was used primarily as a stop-over for summer horse-pack trips, operated by Jim's younger brother Pat, to Sunshine Valley Camp. During the late 1930s into the 1940s, rides to Shadow Lake and Redearth Valley began at the CPR section foreman's house at Massive near Hillsdale meadow then proceeded along Highway 1-A. A small footbridge crossed the Bow River,

*By the 1970s, the original CPR cabin had been painted green, a vestibule added and the almost forgotten link in the CPR's chain of camps was a candidate for demolition, right.*

*Beginning in 1992, the CPR Cabin was completely restored. The interior partitions were removed creating a comfortable lounge, below.*

so riders dismounted and walked over the bridge while the horses were forded across the river.

Sunshine Valley Camp evolved into the Sunshine Valley ski area, one of the major ski resorts in the Canadian Rock-

ies. The tiny rest house near Shadow Lake sat relatively untouched—a nearly forgotten link from the heydays of CPR backcountry development. The Brewster Transport Company continued to lease Shadow Lake into the 1950s, when Bud Brewster took over the lease and property in 1954.

In 1953-54, the Trans Canada Highway was built up the Bow Valley and made all trails along the southwest side of the valley readily accessible, including that to Shadow Lake. During the late 1950s, the rest house was used by Bud and Annette Brewster to accommodate small groups of hikers. As the years passed, many original CPR backcountry facilities were dismantled or converted to other uses.

In 1970, Shadow Lake Rest House was a candidate for demolition, removal or conversion to a warden's cabin. Bud Brewster had other plans in mind, and retained his hold on the property.

The original cabin is one of the "few surviving, well built, log structures following the once popular vernacular building style in the Rocky Mountains," according to a Federal Heritage Building Report.

That report was done prior to approval for renovation and development of Shadow Lake. After a change in parks policy, plans were agreed upon, and the long awaited go-ahead for construction came in 1990. Foundation work for the first six cabins began in August 1991.

What began as a simple log cabin on

*A new dining and kitchen cabin was built in 1994.*

*The original CPR cabin, as seen from the new dining cabin, can be identified by its corbelled logs supporting the porch roof. Shadow Lake Lodge is now a contemporary version of a 1920s backcountry bungalow camp.*

a popular trail is now a complex of twelve new guest-cabins, a staff cabin, the CPR Cabin (the original rest house) and a new kitchen and dining cabin. Today, Bud's daughter Alison Brewster and her husband Byran Niehaus operate Shadow Lake Lodge and Cabins.

The new cabins were designed by Bud Brewster and Niehaus and follow the Standard Plan originated for parks' cabins in 1918. While the cabins reflect historical backcountry construction, building techniques had changed. The days of hauling harvested timber to the site with horses were long gone. Instead, Kooteney Log Homes in British Columbia milled the logs for all of the new structures, and the first loads were flown in by helicopter. By the time construction stopped in October, four walls of each cabin were up.

The following summer, the new cabins were finished and the original CPR Cabin renovated. The cabin was then dark green with white painted log ends, and a plywood vestibule had been added to the front door. Structurally, it was in remarkably good condition, in part, because it had been built on a small stone foundation—unusual for that type of building. The cabin was lifted from its foundation, one rotten sill log replaced, and a new wood floor installed lower than the original floor line. The partitions were removed and interior logs bleached. The original cabin did not have a fireplace, and today a wood-burning stove on a local-stone hearth

*Scenes like Haiduk Peak and Redearth Creek have always drawn visitors to the backcountry of Banff National Park.*

warms the lounge. Thermal pane windows in the exact size and place of the originals were installed and are trimmed with natural wood planking.

Outside, the logs were primed and painted with a clear natural paint to give it a yellow tone (once called CPR yellow), and a new porch was built that complements the stepped log work supporting the porch overhang. The original shingle roof was insulated and covered with a tin roof.

The interior of CPR Cabin illustrates the carefully executed original log work. A ridgepole and eight peeled log purlins run the length of the ceiling with log rafters and plank sheathing. When renovation was completed, the cabin served as the kitchen and dining room while the new dining facility was under construction.

The dining cabin, built in 1994, is designed much as the original rest house. Constructed of milled logs, it is twenty-five by thirty-eight feet. Instead of stepped logs supporting the overhang, two log columns support the verandah roof. The entry is centered and flanked by windows replicating the design of the original cabin. Inside, two crossbeam supports divide the space into thirds. The kitchen is off the back and hearty meals are served at four long tables. Food is prepared on propane stoves, and there is running water in the lounge and kitchen.

In 1995-1997, three more cabins were built. From 1993 on, logs for all construction were brought to the site during the winter by snowmobile rather than helicopter.

The cabins, each named after a surrounding peak, are tucked into the forest along a meadow. As with the CPR's original stop-over cabin plans, they have no bathrooms. Lavatories are outhouses, and washing facilities consist of a bowl and pitcher with buckets of hot water delivered each morning. The guest cabins are heated by propane and feather filled duvets cover the beds.

The compound is obviously much larger than the original rest house built in another era for another use, but the traditional log design and detail are in keeping with historic backcountry plans. Shadow Lake is a backcountry bungalow camp of the 1920s recreated in the 1990s. To Alison Brewster, Shadow Lake Lodge and Cabins is a fitting tribute to her father.

"Shadow Lake is the way it is today because of Bud Brewster. It is his dream. I'm just lucky enough that I came along and am able to run it," says his daughter.

Running the lodge is no small undertaking. Supplies arrive twice a week by horsepack in summer and snowmobile in winter from Redearth parking lot off

*Mount Ball is reflected in the subalpine waters of Shadow Lake.*

the Trans Canada Highway, the same eight-mile route that guests traverse here from the valley floor. Parks Canada no longer allows commercial horses in the area. Instead, because a majority of the trek is on a fire trail, mountain bikes are permitted. But bikes must be left locked at racks before the trail forges into dense forest then opens to a subalpine meadow. Shadow Lake Lodge is a welcome respite, and tea is served from just before noon until five o'clock for day visitors or overnight guests.

Those who stay the night usually spend their days hiking, fishing or cross-country skiing depending on the season, then everyone gathers for dinner. After a delicious meal, they retire to the CPR Cabin for reading, cards or conversation.

Or they can sit on the verandah.

The summer sun sets over Ball Pass illuminating the creek and meadow with Haiduk Peak in the background. Cumulus clouds drift across the sky that glows brightly in the last rays of sunlight. The sun disappears as a full moon rises, and for a brief moment, one can imagine a group of Sky Line Trail Hikers from decades past resting in the same spot and swapping stories of the day's adventures.

I am an American who slipped across the border and experienced the inexplicable joy of the Canadian Rockies and the genuine warmth and enthusiasm of the people.

It is a summer afternoon, and I am supposed to be writing about a charming historic building. Instead, I am mesmerized by a cloud formation as it transforms from a white puff to a silky gray shroud softening the peaks that cut the Continental Divide.

There is a tiny balcony along the second floor of Lake O'Hara Lodge that I had staked out. Everyone of every age is hiking, so the spot is mine, a place where I can calibrate clouds in peace.

Just inside the lodge, a gallery of photographs lines the walls. I study the faces of Catharine and Peter Whyte, Dr. George (Tommy) and Adeline Link, Lawrence Grassi, Lillian Gest and Katie Gardiner, Edward and Walter Feuz. At other lodges or buried in archives there are other faces: Basil Gardom, Jimmy and Billie Simpson, Lizzie Rummel and Erling Strom, the Brewster clan; in each face I see the passion of pioneers. The men and women whose lives seem as rich as mortals' can be. Recluses, artists, writers, outfitters, guides, moun-

*Ken Jones, July 1998*

taineers, skiers and railmen whose voices and stories are embedded here as tightly as the chinking wedged between each log.

People of character, crassness and culture, brains and brawn. Individuals with raw edges and contradictions that kept them from a monochromatic life in the

flat lands. They were men and women who formed an odd and diverse community, and they left us the beneficieries.

There were those who came much earlier, but I like to imagine being with those who made recent history. Author Brian Patton speculates that I just like the gossip.

One of the best days of research for this book was when I happened upon Ken Jones, a small wiry man of eighty-seven chopping wood behind Skoki Lodge. I had read his biography and chuckled over stories of "Jonesy" that Barb Renner shared with me at Mount Assiniboine Lodge. The night before, my husband and I had been listening to tapes of the recollections of Jimmy Simpson, Jr., and Jones at Num-Ti-Jah Lodge where Ken had done the "axe" work. We had left Num-Ti-Jah, then hiked over Deception Pass to Skoki Lodge. As we took our last steps to the porch, I heard that voice. I followed it, and there he was. Amazed, I sat on a bench behind the kitchen and laughed with, listened to and learned from *Ken Jones, Mountain Man*. A bright, charming and accomplished gentlemen, he pointed out purlins, joists and log work that his much younger hands had created, and plucked stories for me from his vast store of memory.

I was fortunate to have met Ken Jones. And anyone who cares about Canadian Rocky Mountain history is fortunate that the Whyte Museum of the Canadian Rockies is in Banff. In the museum's archives, I watched Jon Whyte's video of Jimmy Simpson. Jon's aunt, artist/philanthropist Catharine Whyte, is interviewing the 92-year-old legend at Num-Ti-Jah Lodge in 1971. Jimmy was as eclectic as he was eccentric, and he loved opera. It is the cracking 78 rpm opera recordings in the background that tugs at your heart. "You know, Catharine, I'd like to be young again," he says, then pauses as if to reconsider. "I had a very fine life. I had a real life."

Real is what these people were. Jimmy, Billie, Catharine, Peter, Tommy, Adeline, Lillian, Basil, Lizzie and Erling are all gone, but I know them because they cared enough to leave a legacy. A museum, writing, art, films, tapes, trails and, of course, these buildings.

I chose to write about lodges in the Canadian Rockies because their survival means a link to the people who created, operated or happily frequented them. I can focus on the Rundle rock, hand hewn timbers, peeled logs and

*Banff artists and philanthropists Catharine and Peter Whyte left many legacies; their presence is still felt at places like Skoki Lodge.*

stone fireplaces. I can search for architectural drawings, historical photographs and buried documents and be thrilled by my discoveries.

While this book fills a small historic niche about a massive place, my hope is that Basil, Catharine and Peter, Jimmy and Billie, Tommy and Adeline, Lawrence and Lillian and the rest of

them—those who knew these places because they lived them—would have found my work acceptable.

And that Jon Whyte, whom I never met before his death but feel I know from his extensive writing about the Rockies, would have gleaned one passage from this book that was worthy of reading aloud to friends over a glass of wine.

# SELECTED BIBLIOGRAPHY

## Books

Barrett, Anthony A. and Liscombe, Rhodri Windsor. *Francis Rattenbury and British Columbia: Architecture and Challenge in the Imperial Age* (Vancouver, 1983)

Berton, Pierre, *The Impossible Railway* (New York, 1972)

Djuff, Ray, *The Prince of Wales Hotel* (Waterton, 1991)

Gest, Lillian, *History of Lake O'Hara* (Fourth printed edition, 1991) and *The History of Mount Assiniboine* (1979)

Hart, E.J., *Jimmy Simpson: Legend of the Rockies* (Canadian Rockies/Vancouver, 1991) and *The Selling of Canada: The CPR and the Beginnings of Canadian Tourism* (Banff, 1983) and *The Brewster Story* (Banff, 1981)

Kalman, Harold, *A History of Canadian Architecture*, Vols. I & II (Toronto, New York, Oxford, 1994) and *The Railway Hotels and the Development of the Chateau Style in Canada* (University of Victoria, 1968)

Kariel, Herbert G. and Patricia E., *Alpine Huts in the Selkirks, Rockies, and Purcells* (Banff, 1986)

Lothian, W.F., *A History of Canada's National Parks* (Parks Canada, 1981)

Marty, Sid, *A Grand and Fabulous Notion: The First Century of Canada's Parks* (Toronto, 1984)

Outram, James, *In the Heart of the Canadian Rockies* (New York, 1906)

Patton, Brian, ed. by Jon Whyte, *Mountain Chronicles* (Banff, 1992)

Patton, Brian & Robinson, Bart, *The Canadian Rockies Trail Guides* (Banff, Sixth edition, 1994)

Pratte, France Gagnon, *The Banff Springs Hotel: The Castle in the Rockies* (Quebec, 1997)

Robinson, Bart, *Banff Springs: The Story of a Hotel* (Banff, 1988)

Sandford, R.W., *The Canadian Alps: The History of Mountaineering in Canada*, Volume 1 (Banff, 1990)

Smith, Cyndi, *Jasper Park Lodge: In the Heart of the Canadian Rockies* (Canmore, 1985)

Stevens, G.R., *History of the Canadian National Railway* (New York, London, 1973)

Strom, Erling, *Pioneers on Skis* (New York, 1977)

Tetarenko, Lorne & Kim, *Ken Jones: Mountain Man* (Calgary, 1996)

Vaughan, Walter, *The Life and Work of Sir William Van Horne* (New York, 1920)

Wilcox, Walter Dwight, *The Rockies of Canada* (New York, 1900)

Whyte, Jon, *Tommy and Lawrence: The Ways and the Trails of Lake O'Hara* (The Lake O'Hara Trails Club, 1983)

Whyte, Jon, ed. *Pete 'n' Catharine: Their Story* (Banff, 1980)

Whyte, Jon and Harmon, Carole, *Lake Louise: A Diamond in the Wilderness* (Banff, 1982)

Whyte, Jon and Edward Cavell, *Mountain Glory: The Art of Peter and Catharine Whyte* (Banff, 1988)

## Reports

B.C. Heritage Conservation Branch, "The Mount Assiniboine Provincial Park Lodge," unpublished report (1986)

DeJong, James, "Banff Springs Hotel, Spray Avenue, Banff, Alberta," Historic Sites and Monuments Board of Canada Agenda Paper (1988)

Department of the Interior (Canada), "Annual Reports." Ottawa: Pub. by Gov. of Canada, 1887-1918

Doherty, Johanna H., "Shadow Lake Rest House, Banff National Park," Federal Heritage Bureau Review Office, Building Report: 87-133 (1987)

Mills, Edward, "Heritage Character Statement, Prince of Wales Hotel." Heritage Canada, Parks Canada (January 1994)

——, "Lake O'Hara Lodge, Yoho National Park, British Columbia," Federal Heritage Buildings Review Office, Building Report: 93-105 (1993)

——, "Rustic Building Programs in Canada's National Parks 1887-1950, Part I & II," Parks Canada, WRO Historical Services (Nov. 1992)

Mills, G.E. and Taylor, C.J., "Jasper National Park, Planning Program for Jasper Park Lodge Redevelopment—Planning Framework," Parks Canada (August 1990)

——; Taylor, C.J.; Buchik, Pat, "Jasper National Park, Jasper Park Lodge: Built Heritage Resource Description and Analysis," Canadian Parks Service technical report (April 1992)

MacFarland, Kate, "Skoki Ski Lodge National Historic Site (Six Buildings), Banff National Park, Alberta," Federal Heritage Buildings Review Office, Report: 96-105 (1996)

Parks Canada Western Service Centre (prepared by), Calgary, "Four Mountain Parks Outlying Commercial Accommodations, Heritage Character Statements" (August 1997)

Richard Friesen and Associates, "Banff, Jasper, Kootenay, Yoho and National Parks: Outlying Historic Buildings Data Base," Ottawa: Environment Canada Parks (1985)

Sumpter, Ian D. and Perry, W., "Archaeological Resource Impact Assessments Yoho National Park," Series No. 385 Ottawa: Parks Canada (1987)

Taylor, C.J., "Lake Louise, Built Heritage Resource Description & Analysis," Parks Canada, Calgary (1998)

## Articles

Barr, Ferree, "A Talk with Bruce Price," *Architectural Record,* Great American Architects Series, No. 5, June 1899, p. 81

Lady Agnes, "An Unconventional Holiday," *The Ladies Home Journal,* August 1891 and September 1891

Mills, Edward, "The Bungalow Trail, Rustic Railway Bungalow Camps in Canada's National Parks," *Bulletin,* Society for the Study of Architecture in Canada (Sept./Dec., 1993), p. 60

Rogatnik, Abraham, "Canadian Castles: Phenomenon of the Railway Hotel," *Architectural Review,* CXLI (May 1967), pp 364-372

"Sketch for a Hotel" (Banff Springs Hotel), *Building* VI, Feb. 26, 1887

Sturgis, Russell, "A Review of the Works of Bruce Price," *Architectural Record*, Great American Architects Series, No. 5, June 1889

## Archives

**Canadian Pacific Corporate Archives, Montreal, Quebec**

"Building a Twelve-Story Concrete Structure in Zero Weather," *Railway Age,* June 27, 1925

Canadian Pacific Railway, *Bulletin* 123A, April 1, 1919

Executive Correspondence files from July 5, 1892 to August 18, 1925

Evans, E.W., "Chateau Lake Louise," *Construction*, April 1926

Brochure Collection: "Guide to Lake Louise with Map," circa 1912; "Canadian Pacific Christmas," 1923; MacBeth, Madge, "Emerald Lake British Columbia," Canadian Pacific Rockies, 1924; "Bungalow Camps in the Canadian Pacific Rockies," 1926 & 1927; "What to do at…Emerald Lake Chalet and Nearby Lodges," Canadian Pacific Hotels in the Canadian Rockies, 1929, 1930 & 1946 editions; "O'Hara Bungalow Camp," Canadian Pacific Rockies, 1927; "Emerald Lake Chalet," Canadian Pacific Railway, 1931; "Resorts in the Rockies," Canadian Pacific, 1931

Extensive use of Public Relations and Advertising photography files

**Glenbow Archives, Calgary, Alberta**

Canadian Pacific Railway—Hotel Department, Hotel Department Series, 1901-1953, Records No. M7588, PD 240, NA 4465

**Jasper Yellowhead Museum & Archives, Jasper, Alberta**

Info Files: Hotels, Motels, Etc., Jasper Park Lodge:

*Canadian National Railways Magazine*: "Natural Beauties of Jasper National Park," May 1922; "Jasper Park the Ideal Resort For Tourists to the Rocky Mountains," July 1923; "Earl Haig Opens Jasper Golf Course," August 1925; "Jasper Park Lodge, a Quarter of a Century," June 1948

*Edmonton Journal*, July 15, 1952, "Jasper Park Lodge Burns To Ground"

"Jasper Park Lodge, The Main Building," unattributed clipping, 1978

*Lethridge* [Alberta] *Herald*; July 17, 1952, "A Disastrous Fire"

McDonough, Tom, "Creation and Development of Jasper Park Lodge, Canadian National Railways" (circa 1960)

**Minnesota Historical Society, St. Paul, Minnesota**

Great Northern Railway, 22.F.119(B), Glacier Park Co., Canadian Division, File 22.F.9.7(B); Presidents file, 132.F.19.5(B) and photographic files

**Whyte Museum of the Canadian Rockies, Banff, Alberta**

Black, Carol, "Skoki Lodge," unpublished manuscript (1984)

Canadian National Railways: report, notes and photographs, Record No. M54/V57

Canadian Pacific Railway brochures, Banff Springs Hotel in

the Canadian Rockies, 1967 and undated editions
Chateau Lake Louise, Record No. M180
*The Contract Record*: "The Construction of an Open Air Concrete Swimming Pool in the Canadian Rockies," April 1916; and "Reinforced Concrete in Theory and Practice," "Swimming Pool and Bath House at C.P.R. Banff Springs Hotel," 1930
*Crag and Canyon*: "Banff Springs Hotel," June 24, 1901; "The New Chateau Lake Louise," June 26, 1925; "Canadian Pacific Construction," March 8, 1926; "North Wing C.P.R. Banff Springs Hotel Prey to Fire," April 9, 1926
Getty, Ian Allison Ludlow, "A Historical Guide to Yoho National Park," File 70/5R2.12, Contract No. WR 191/71 (June 1972)
Harrison, Nellie, oral history: "Human History of Yoho National Park," January 1970
"Jimmy Simpson: Mountain Man," Filmwest Association (1970-71), produced by Jon Whyte
Lake O'Hara Lodge, Records No. M127/V342
"Our Wild Westland," *The Dominion Illustrated*, Sept. 1889
Photography files
Simpson, Jimmy, CBC audio tapes M75/V118/57/2 (A-V)
Simpson, James, letters to J. Monroe Thorington, published as "Days Remembered," The American Alpine Journal, 1974
Skoki Lodge fonds—1943-1993, Record No. M145
Strom, Erling, oral history, S1/23 (A-C)
Trail Riders of the Canadian Rockies, Bulletin No. 20, May 1929
Whyte, Peter and Catharine fonds, Oct. 8, 1930 letter, M36/84; Feb. 14, 1932, M36/87

**Provincial Archives of British Columbia, Victoria, BC**
Parks and Outdoor Recreation on Mount Assiniboine Provincial Park, GR-1991, B-1748, File No. 2-3-2-1, Sections 1, 2, 3, and 4

**National Archives of Canada, Ottawa, Ontario**
RG 84:
T-9394, Vol. 2247, Y16-21, Yoho National Park, Twin Falls Tea House, 1922-28
T-9407, Vol. 522, J17-GTP-5, Part I, Jasper Park, 1909-1912
T-9407, Vol. 522, J17-GTP-2, Part I, Letter to HR Charlton, 26 Feb. 1915 and letter to RH Charlton to JB Harkin, 19 March 1915
T-9408, Vol. 523, J17-6tp-8, Part I, RH Campbell to Frank Oliver, 4 April 1911
T-9408, Vol. 523, J17-GTP-8, M. Hays to Frank Oliver, 30 March 1911
T-9411, Vol. 661, File B16-41, Part I & II, Banff National Park, Bow Lake, Num-Ti-Gah Lodge, 1919-1957
T-9413, Vol. 666, file B16-88, Banff National Park, Abbots Pass, Six Glacier Resthouse, CPR, 1923-27
T-9414, Vols. 665, 666, 667, Files B16-94 & B16-100, Shadow Lake Rest House, Sunshine Valley
T-9416, Vol. 671, File B16-107, Shadow Lake, Skoki Ski Camp
T-9445, Vol. 701, B16-135, Part I, CPR to Dept. of Interior, 22 Nov. 1911
T-9605, Vol. 920, B24-1-1 to 6, Part I JB Harking to Ewart,

Scott, MacLaren and Kelly, 19 Feb. 1914
T-9623 Vol. 1478, J16-29, Parts I & 3, Jasper National Park, Jasper Park Lodge plans 1926 (complete file)
T-9891, Vol. 2244, Y16-17, Part I, Yoho National Park, 1921-53
T-9894, Vol. 2247, Y16-21, Twin Falls Tea House
T-9894 and T-9895, Vol. 2248, Y16-26, Part I, Yoho National Park, Lake O'Hara, 1923-56
T-9896, Vol. 2249, File Y16-41, Parts I & II Yoho National Park, 1902-1953

## Other

Gardom, Basil, notes from unpublished memoirs to his son, Garde B. Gardom, written circa 1955, courtesy of The Honourable Garde B. Gardom, Q.C., Lieutenant-Governor of British Columbia
Jones, Ken, and Simpson, Jimmy, Jr., interviews audiotaped at Num-Ti-Jah Lodge, April 3, 1998, courtesy of Num-Ti-Jah Lodge
Oland, Douglas, personal memoirs, courtesy of the Oland family, Waterton, Alberta
Renner, Barb, personal photographic files, Canmore, Alberta

# PHOTOGRAPH & ILLUSTRATION CREDITS

## Color Photography

**Fred Pflughoft & David Morris,** pages: title page, 4-5, 20, 21, 27, 29, 30, 33, 35, 45, 47, 49, 54 (left, top & bottom), 59 (left), 60 (top), 61, 69 (lower), 71 (lower), 81, 83, 84, 89, 92, 94, 95 (right), 101,102 (top), 104, 106, 119, 120, 121 (top right), 134, 136, 137, 142 (top), 144, 147, 153, 154
**David Morris,** pages: 14, 16-17, 37, 41, 60 (lower left), 62 (lower left), 64, 67, 71 (top), 72, 74-75, 76, 82 (lower), 93 (lower), 95 (left), 102 (lower), 105, 112, 118, 121 (top left; lower left & right), 145 (lower), 146, 148, 149, 157, 159, 164
**Fred Pflughoft,** pages: 2-3, 18, 24-25 (fold out), 25, 36, 38, 48, 50, 54 (lower right), 56, 59 (right), 62 (upper & lower, right), 63, 72-73, 80, 82 (top), 84-85, 86, 89 (fold out), 93 (upper), 96, 103, 108-109, 110-111, 115, 116 117, 126, 128, 132-133, 138, 141, 142 (left), 143, 145 (top), 150, 155, 156
**Courtesy, Banff Springs Hotel,** page 31
**Jerry Barnes,** pages 135, 158
**Russ Heinel Group,** Sidney, BC, page 122
**Brian Patton,** page 140

## Historic Photos & Drawings

**Canadian Pacific Archives, Montreal, Quebec,** pages: 6, No. NS 1960; 8, No. A 6510; 9, No. NS 2395; 11, No. B 6531-1; 12, No. NS 6689; 13, No. BR 176; 15, (right) No. 3A 6164; 32, (top) No. M.3 and (lower) No. A 6189; 46, No. NS 7756; 90, (top) No. NS 16537 and (lower) No. NS 12027; 114, No. NS 7806 and (inset) No. NS 24831; 140, Nicholas

Morant photo, M. 1950
**Canadian National Railway Archives, Ottawa, Ontario,** page 52, CN 16703
**Garde B.Gardom personal collection, Victoria, BC,** pages: 15 (left); 42
**Glacier Natural History Association, West Glacier, Montana,** pages: 68, Hileman collection 6514; 69, Hileman collection 132.F.19.5 (B)
**Glenbow Archives, Calgary, Alberta,** pages: 28 (left), Banff Springs Hotel, central tower addition, W.S. Painter, nd, D4880-6, and (right) Banff Springs Hotel, new south wing, east elevation, J.W. Orrock, 1926, P-4880; 46, Chateau Lake Louise, section and end elevation, Sept. 1924, Barrot and Blackader, P-4800-4; 62, PD-3-3811; 78, Emerald Lake Hotel, February 1902, P-6880; 88, Lake O'Hara Log Chalet, Dec. 1925, P-4880-8; 124, Abbot's Hut, P-4880-10; 126, Proposed Rest House Plain of Six Glaciers, P-4880-12
**Jasper Park Lodge collection, Jasper National Park, Alberta** page 57, (top) V-36-6, (middle) V-47-19
**Jasper Yellowhead Museum and Archives, Jasper, Alberta,** page, 53, 994.56.1462a
**Lake O'Hara Lodge collection, Yoho National Park, BC,** pages: 91, 94
**National Archives of Canada, Ottawa, Ontario,** pages: 98, RG84 A-2-A, Vol. 661, File B-16-41, Reel T-9411; 100, Neg. No. C146030; 152, RG84 T-9416, Vol. 671, File B16-107
National Library of Canada, Ottawa, Ontario, page 53, NL 13574
**Parks Canada, Calgary, Alberta and Jasper National Park, Alberta,** pages: 55; 57, (Le Pub) NWJ30/B1/Roll J-22; 58, (Special Cabin) NW J30/R1/4 /6/Roll J22; 60, (Greenhouses & gardeners' dwelling) 38500101; 66, (Prince of Wales Hotel) WL95R4 1 of 12;
**Shadow Lake Lodge collection, Banff National Park, Alberta,** page 153 (lower)
**Whyte Museum of the Canadian Rockies, Banff, Alberta,** pages: 22, V92/NG3-1; 23, M282; 26, Byron Harmon collection, V263/NG11-13; 43, Feuz, Edward, 1884-1981 collection, V200, NA66-1865; 44, V573 NA66-2174; 78, Byron Harmon collection, V263/5229; 79, Byron Harmon collection, V263 NA71-5231; 99, (top) V577-PD-24 and (lower) V469-1001; 125, (inset) V200/NA66-1283 and V200/PA44-81A; 127, George Noble photo, V469/2590; 130, V79 NA66-1116; 131, (top) Peter Whyte photo, V683/I.C.I.a.i. Box 35 and (lower) V79 NA66-1117; 142, V227/3392

## Illustration

**Dave Ember,** pages: 21, 39, 51, 65, 77, 87, 97, 113, 123, 129, 139, 151
**Linda McCray,** page 7, inside back cover

## Map

**Linda McCray,** end pages

Mount Victoria rises above Lake Louise, and its namesake Chateau is dwarfed by the setting.

Map of **Great Lodges** of the **Canadian Rockies**

1. Banff Springs Hotel
2. Chateau Lake Louise
   Plain of Six Glaciers Teahouse
3. Jasper Park Lodge
4. Prince of Wales Hotel
5. Emerald Lake Lodge
6. Lake O'Hara Lodge
7. Num-Ti-Jah
8. Twin Falls Chalet
9. Abbott Pass Hut
10. Skoki Lodge
11. Mt. Assiniboine Lodge
12. Shadow Lake Lodge